AND FURTHERMORE

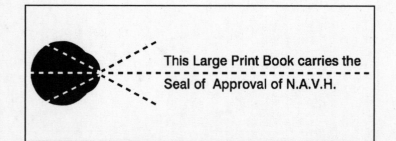

This Large Print Book carries the
Seal of Approval of N.A.V.H.

AND FURTHERMORE

JUDI DENCH

as told to John Miller

THORNDIKE PRESS
A part of Gale, Cengage Learning

GALE
CENGAGE Learning

Detroit • New York • San Francisco • New Haven, Conn • Waterville, Maine • London

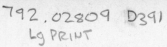

GALE
CENGAGE Learning™

LIBRARY OF CONGRESS CATALOGING-IN-PUBLICATION DATA

Dench, Judi, 1934–
    And furthermore / by Judi Dench as told to John Miller.
        p. cm. — (Thorndike Press large print biography)
    ISBN-13: 978-1-4104-3863-8 (hardcover)
    ISBN-10: 1-4104-3863-5 (hardcover)
    1. Dench, Judi, 1934– 2. Actors—Great Britain—Biography. 3.
Large type books. I. Title.
PN2598.D447A3 2011b
792.0'28092—dc22
    [B]   2011012847

Published in 2011 by arrangement with St. Martin's Press, LLC.

Printed in the United States of America
1 2 3 4 5 6 7 15 14 13 12 11

For Finty and Sammy

CONTENTS

LIST OF ILLUSTRATIONS

Unless otherwise credited, all pictures belong to Judi Dench. While every effort has been made to contact copyright holders, if any have been inadvertently overlooked the publishers would be happy to acknowledge them in future editions.

TEXT ILLUSTRATIONS

11

liams / Art and Commerce)

340   As Judith Bliss in *Hay Fever*, 2006 (Nigel Norrington / ArenaPal) 1074229

356   As Titania in *A Midsummer Night's Dream*, 2010 (Nobby Clark / ArenaPal)

PHOTO INSERT

As the First Fairy in *A Midsummer Night's Dream*, 1957 (Snowdon / Camera Press)

On holiday in France in the 1950s

As Maria in *Twelfth Night*, 1958 (Mander & Mitchenson Archive / ArenaPal)

As the Princess of France in *The Age of Kings*, 1960 (BBC Photo Library)

In *Z-Cars*, 1960 (BBC Photo Library)

With Franco Zeffirelli rehearsing for *Romeo and Juliet*, 1960 (Getty)

With Peggy Ashcroft in *The Cherry Orchard*, 1961 (ArenaPal)

Charity dancing photo, 1963 (Reg Lancaster / Express / Getty)

As Titania in *A Midsummer Night's Dream*, 1962 (Express / Getty)

As Isabella in *Measure for Measure*, 1962 (Gordon Goode / Shakespeare Birthplace Trust)

As St Joan, 1966

With Ian Richardson in Peter Hall's *A Midsummer Night's Dream*, 1965

As Sally Bowles in *Cabaret,* 1968 (Hulton Archive / Getty)

As Perdita in *The Winter's Tale,* 1969 (Hulton Archive / Getty)

As Viola in *Twelfth Night* with Donald Sinden as Malvolio, 1969 (Morris Newcombe)

Wedding Day, 6 February 1971 (Bentley Archive / Getty)

Michael in Judi's going-away hat

Rehearsing with Michael (John Brook)

With Michael in *London Assurance,* 1970 (Mander & Mitchenson Archive / ArenaPal)

With Michael in *The Merchant of Venice,* 1971 (John Brook)

With Finty as a baby (Press Association)

Michael and Finty in Cyprus

Finty in her communion outfit

As Lady Macbeth with Ian McKellen, 1976 (Laurence Burns / ArenaPal)

With Jeremy Irons in *Langrishe, Go Down,* 1978 (SUS / Camera Press)

Rehearsing *Much Ado About Nothing,* 1976 (Nobby Clark)

With Norman Rodway in *Juno and the Paycock,* 1980 (Donald Cooper / Photostage)

With Anna Massey in *A Kind of Alaska,* 1982 (Laurence Burns)

With Michael in *A Pack of Lies,* 1983

(Donald Cooper / Photostage)

With Michael in *Mr and Mrs Nobody,* 1986 (Donald Cooper / Photostage)

The cast of BBC Radio 3's *King Lear,* 1984 (Topfoto)

A trip to a brewery for *Entertaining Strangers,* 1987

The black glove (Tim Pigott-Smith)

As Cleopatra in *Antony and Cleopatra,* 1987 (Donald Cooper / Photostage)

As Gertrude with Daniel Day-Lewis as Hamlet, 1989 (Donald Cooper / Photostage)

With Michael Pennington in *The Gift of the Gorgon,* 1992 (Ben Christopher / Arena-Pal)

As Christine Foskett in *Absolute Hell,* 1995 (ArenaPal)

Backstage preparing for *Amy's View,* 1997 (John Timbers)

Rehearsing for *A Little Night Music,* 1995 (Sasha Gusov / ArenaPal)

Rehearsing for *Amy's View* with Richard Eyre and David Hare, 1997 (John Haynes)

With Michael at John Mills's eightieth birthday party, 1988

Enjoying the garden at home

Michael

Finty and Sammy

Michael and Sammy at Eriska

With Sammy, Finty and Minnie (John Timbers)

With Geoffrey Palmer in *As Time Goes By* (BBC Photo Library)

With members of the cast of *Cranford* (BBC Photo Library)

With Pierce Brosnan in *Die Another Day,* 2002 (Topfoto)

With Daniel Craig in *Casino Royale,* 2006 (Jay Maidment / Eon / Danjaq / Sony / The Kobal Collection)

With Tom Stoppard and John Madden after the announcement of the Oscar nominations for *Shakespeare in Love* (Topfoto)

With the Oscar, 1999 (Getty)

In Italy filming *Tea with Mussolini,* 1999

With Kevin Spacey

With Bob Hoskins in *Mrs Henderson Presents,* 2005 (Stephen Frears)

With Toby Stephens in *The Royal Family,* 2001 (ArenaPal)

With Bill Clinton and Maggie Smith after a performance of *The Breath of Life,* 2002

With Maggie Smith in *Ladies in Lavender,* 2004 (Tom Collins / Scala Productions / The Kobal Collection)

With Jim Broadbent in *Iris,* 2001 (Miramax Films / Topfoto)

With Cate Blanchett in *Notes on a Scandal,* 2005 (Giles Keyte / Fox Searchlight / The

Kobal Collection)
In *Nine,* 2010 (Lucamar Productions / The Kobal Collection)
In *Rage,* 2008
At the Prom to celebrate Stephen Sondheim's eightieth birthday, 31 July 2010 (Yui Mok / Press Association)

PREFACE

I do not consider this an autobiography. I have neither the time nor the skill to write one, and John Miller has covered much of my life in his 1998 biography, the seventieth birthday book from my friends which he edited, and the illustrated *Scenes from my Life* we assembled together.

So when Ion Trewin approached me about this new volume I hesitated for a long while. Eventually he persuaded me that told in my own voice, filling gaps and remembering much that John Miller did not know or did not include in his biography, was more than sufficient justification for a new and updated account.

I said that I supposed in that case we might entitle it *And Furthermore,* as a follow-up to those earlier books. I hasten to add that this is also not the final word, since I have often expressed the wish to emulate my dear friends and mentors, John Gielgud and Peggy Ashcroft, both of whom continued working right to the end.

I have enjoyed — and am still enjoying — a wonderful life, and made some friendships I cherish deeply, many of which appear in these pages, and that is one of the most important reasons why I am happy to put all this on the record.

■ ■ ■ ■

1
EARLY DAYS
1934–1957

■ ■ ■ ■

I can hardly believe that it is more than half a century since I first stepped on to the stage of the Old Vic Theatre, and into a way of life that has brought me the most rewarding professional relationships and friendships. I cannot imagine now ever doing anything else with my life except acting, but it was not something that I actually planned when I was growing up. That may seem strange, as my whole family was deeply involved in theatre in one way or another.

My father was a doctor in general practice, but spent much of his spare time acting with the Settlement Players, a very good amateur group in York. He and my mother were keen theatregoers, so my elder brothers and I were taken to the theatre from a very early age. When I saw the celebrated farce *Cuckoo in the Nest* by Ben Travers, I laughed so much when a man jumped up in a laundry basket at the end of a bed wearing those combinations they called longjohns, that I thought I would have some kind of fit. In fact I think my mother must have decided that I really was going to have a fit, because I was taken home at the interval, and only brought back the next night to see the second half of the play. We went to *Peter Pan* at Leeds, and when we came home I said, 'Couldn't we fix some wires up in the waiting room, and I could come flying in from the consulting room to the waiting room?' My parents must have been in despair.

Daddy was a fine actor, and a marvellous after-dinner speaker; with a great sense of timing. He had the ease of an Irishman in telling stories, and he had a brilliant sense of humour. He was actually born in Dorset, but brought up in Dublin, and only moved to York after he married. He was so very grounded as a doctor. I used to go visiting patients with him, and as he turned into roads the children used to come and hold on to the car. He became really very popular as a GP, and we hardly ever saw him at any meals, because he was always out delivering babies. People still come up to me and say, 'You won't believe this, but your father delivered me as a baby.' I always try to look surprised.

Mummy also acted occasionally, but more often was responsible for the costumes. Once they went to a party with Daddy as Shakespeare and Mummy as Elizabeth I, and she made the most incredible dress for the Queen. They were also in a film about Dick Turpin's ride to York, and I still have the picture of the two of them on the stairs at home. A man called Wilson, who taught me to ride, was in the film with them, and he left us a box of costumes from it, with various bodices and skirts.

Mummy could whip up anything, and after I had seen the Laurence Olivier film of *Henry V* I longed to go to a fancy-dress party as the Princess of France, so she made me the most beautiful dress, with cotton-wool all round the sleeve marked like ermine. I made the headdress that I had seen Renée Asherson wearing, with a piece of netting round my head and a ruler through the top. It looked absolutely terrific. (It never crossed my mind that one day I would play that part onstage.) Over the years there were all sorts of things that had just got put in the ottoman, which we were always digging through; I just thought that all families got dressed up like that.

When the Settlement Players did Christopher Fry's *The Firstborn* I played Tuesret, the pharaoh's daughter. Christopher became a great friend years later, and I rather regret that is the only time I have ever acted in one of his plays. When I was at Clifton Preparatory School we did a Nativity Play and I was told I was to play a fairy, which I was quite cross about, because I knew the Nativity story did not involve fairies. I also played a snail once, and Alice in *Alice in Wonderland.*

My brothers, Peter and Jeffery, who were quite a bit older than me, appeared in school productions at St Peter's in York, which is one of the oldest schools in the country. In Shaw's *Caesar and Cleopatra* Peter played Caesar and Jeff was Cleopatra. I saw Jeff as Kate in *The Taming of the Shrew* and Cassius in *Julius Caesar,* and Peter as Duncan in *Macbeth.* I thought it was very racy to spin round on the piano stool at home and say, 'What bloody man is that?' That was all I remembered of the play, but I did say that rather a lot.

Because of the age-gap between us I was of course sent to bed much earlier than the boys, and I remember so well going to bed and hearing them playing cricket in the garden, and hearing all that life going on outside; I simply couldn't bear it, and it is still like that. I don't like missing anything, even today I hate to be in bed and hear people talking downstairs, because I am far too nosy, I *have* to know what they are on about.

Our house was in an area called 'York Without', because it was outside the city walls. We had a long straight strip of garden, with a few apple trees. We couldn't grow very much, apart from some lovely lilies-of-the-valley and a few roses, and we used to rake the pears off the tree next door. At the end of the garden was an old barn, and owls used to live in there. When the boys had friends round playing cricket they were always knocking the ball over into Miss Lazenby's garden, and she would never give the ball back, however much we asked for it. One day Jeff found a rat in the barn, and they did it all up and gave it to me to take it round and push through her door. Daddy heard about it, and told us all off.

My first school, Miss Meaby's, was just up the road from my brothers' school, St Peter's, so when I finished for the day I used to go and sit on the wall to watch the boys playing games, waiting for my mother to come and take us home.

When I went to the Mount School in the city there were no such things as day-girls, so I had to be a boarder all the time, but I didn't mind that at all really. We were allowed home at weekends for just a day, but not to sleep. When games were cancelled we had to go on what was called a 'wet-walk', all sorts of different walks that we had to do. So I used to go out of school, ring up home, and they would come and fetch us. We would have a huge tea, then Mummy would water us in the garden with a watering-can, drop us at a corner near school, and we trudged back soaked to the skin. I don't think we were ever caught out.

The first play I saw at the Mount was *Julius Caesar,* with lots of big girls in bigger togas. I thought that was not at all a good play to do, and it is the one Roman play I have fought shy of ever since. But it was there that I first played Titania in *A Midsummer Night's Dream,* a role I returned to with the RSC in 1962 for Peter Hall, and again in 2010 at his request at the Kingston Rose Theatre.

The teacher who had the most influence on me had been known as Joy Harvey when she had worked with John Gielgud, but at school she was called Mrs Macdonald. Her marriage had broken up, but after I left she wrote me the most lovely letter, saying that she was standing on York Station when suddenly her husband had appeared and they had got together again, years after their break-up. She seemed to me quite dissipated; she used to drink, and smoked like a chimney, but she would suddenly talk about acting in the professional theatre, and bring it all alive. She was a good laugher, but she took it very seriously, and she was a terrific teacher.

That is why I have reservations about drama students being taught by people who have never actually worked in the theatre. It has worked sometimes, for actors like John Neville and Richard Burton, but most people need somebody to tell them what it is actually like to be in a company, how you should behave, and the homework you must do, so that you don't take up a lot of other people's time.

The other teacher at the Mount who influenced me was Phoebe Brook, the art mistress. Everybody was encouraged, in whatever they did, to do it well but not to compete. Although we swam and played other sports against other schools, winning was not the important thing. That is quite important in my book. Deep down, I suppose I don't really approve of the awards business, even when I have won them, because you can't really award prizes for acting. That is not to say that when I have won awards I haven't been absolutely thrilled — I have — but I suspect deep down that it is something that goes a bit against the grain. Acting is such a personal, imperfect kind of art.

Acting was just one of the things I did at school; I originally wanted to be a ballet dancer, until Daddy said, 'Well, if you do take up dancing, by the time you are forty you'll have to teach or something, because you just can't go on for ever, it is quite a short career.' I wouldn't have liked that. I don't like the thought of anything packing up.

For a while I wanted to be a theatre designer, and actually went to art school for several months, but then I was taken to see Michael Redgrave as King Lear at Stratford in the early Fifties, and came face to face with a theatre without a curtain. I was only used to a proscenium arch with a curtain, where they changed the set behind it in the interval. Suddenly here was this huge open stage with no curtain at all, just this enormous rough stone that was a throne at the beginning, and turned to become a hovel or a cave, or anything else that was needed. The set was designed by the team of Robert Colquhoun and Robert MacBryde, and I sat there thinking I could never ever have the imagination to do a set like that, and overnight I thought, I don't think I can be the kind of designer I want to be. It really was a kind of road to Damascus for me.

When I was seventeen at the Mount School, Canon Purvis did a new translation of the York Cycle of Mystery Plays, for its first revival since the fifteenth century, produced by Martin Browne, who specialised in religious dramas. He came to the Mount and asked for people to play angels, so we were all taken from school and auditioned; eight of us were chosen, and I got the part of a forgetful angel. I was meant to forget everything, and I did of course forget everything; people used to get so irritated with me. We had all-white robes with a gold collar and gold wigs.

Three years later, in 1954, I played the young man in white clothing sitting at the door of the tomb, or rather in my case not sitting, as Henzie Raeburn (Martin Browne's wife, who was playing Mary Magdalene) insisted that I could perfectly well crouch there while the three Marys did their scene. It actually looked quite angelic, as when I got up there was no chair to be seen. Mummy made the costumes again, Daddy played Annas the High Priest, Caiaphas was the drama teacher John Kay who

31

taught at Bootham's, the Mount's brother school, Joseph O'Conor played Christ, John van Eyssen the Devil, David Giles the Archangel Gabriel, and Tenniel Evans was the Archangel Michael. Mary Ure, who was in the sixth form at the Mount then, played the Virgin Mary. Three years after that, just as I was leaving drama school, Martin Browne asked me to go back and play Eve, but when I got there he said he had changed his mind and wanted me to play the Virgin Mary. Funnily enough, I followed Mary Ure in another part after a three-year gap at Stratford. She was Titania in Peter Hall's production of *The Dream* in 1959, and I played her when he revived it in 1962 with a mostly new cast.

All three productions were done in the open air at St Mary's Abbey, and I was always rained on. It was fine for the Creation of the World, and everything was terrific for the Fall of Lucifer, but when I came on for the Birth of Christ, it just poured down. I used to bend over when he was born, and then come up and part the straw to show the baby, and as I came up I saw people pulling their macs on and putting up umbrellas, and it seemed to happen every time, but it was still a wonderful experience.

Having abandoned my first two ideas of a

career — dancing or designing — it is hardly surprising that I settled on acting, which was entirely due to my brother Jeff. Peter had followed in Daddy's footsteps and gone off to study medicine, but Jeff only ever wanted to be an actor. He didn't talk me into it, but it was his stories of the fun he was having at the Central School of Speech and Drama (to give it its full title just this once) that inspired me. Our parents only ever encouraged us in anything we wanted to do, but my father did say, 'You've got to get your O- and A-levels, because it's a very precarious life. You might have to think about something else at some time, so for goodness' sake work hard. By all means go to Central, if that's what you want to do, but you've got to get those exams.' I got my A-levels in Art and English Literature, though Daddy still had to pay the fees at Central for both of us.

The audition was a written exercise, and I had tonsillitis at the time, so they sent it to me to complete at home. The question paper asked a lot about Greek theatre, which fortunately I had learnt about, though I have always taken care not to appear in any of those plays in the years since: I don't fancy playing in a mask.

The Central School was still based at the

Albert Hall in my day, only moving to Swiss Cottage in North London after I left. We used to cut some lectures and creep into the Albert Hall to listen to people like the great Italian tenor Beniamino Gigli rehearsing. Alfred Hitchcock was filming some scenes from *The Man Who Knew Too Much* in 1955, and one morning we went in and James Stewart was walking towards us, dragging his mac behind him, and said 'Good morning' to us, while we were all completely flattened against the wall. Nobody went to any lectures that day, we all stayed to watch.

I had a lovely time at Central. I stayed right across the road at a hostel run by Charis Fry, daughter of the cricketer C.B. Fry, next to the Royal College of Organists, so there were a lot of musicians and actors living there. It was only a four-minute walk to Central in the morning, and I saw every play in London during those three years. I was there with Jeremy Kemp, Philip Bond (father of Samantha Bond), Ian Hendry, Julian Belfrage (who became my agent), Vanessa Redgrave, Rowena Cooper, and Jenny Daniel (with whom I shared a room).

For the first year we weren't allowed to open our mouths, we just learnt to do a lot of breathing exercises and the Alexander

Technique. Clifford Turner taught us dialect, and although he couldn't do an accent he was a brilliant voice-teacher, and so was Cicely Berry, with whom I have worked throughout my career. I used to adore movement classes with Maggie Rubell, leaping about all over the place, learning relaxation and co-ordination of the body. Nobody ever cured me of falling over, however, which I still have a habit of doing on first nights.

That marvellous old actor Walter Hudd, who was Head of Drama, told us that at some point we would be asked to do a mime, and we wouldn't know when it was coming, but we had better be prepared. Well of course it flew straight out of my head, and then one morning we were all sitting there, and Walter said, 'Right, this is the morning of the mime.'

I thought, The mime? The mime! Good grief! And then Walter called me up first. I could still do it now. I thought that this could only be minimalist. I will walk into a garden that I had been in a very long time ago. So I bent down and picked something and smelt it, then I picked up a stone and threw it into a pool, and just stood there watching the pool, and then I sat on a swing, and that was all I did. At the end of all the mimes Walter gave me top marks, to my astonishment. 'You're like a little Renoir,' he said to me. I will never forget it. I got this fantastic notice from him, and it was in my report at the end of the year. So suddenly I thought that perhaps there is something in this, I do really badly want to do this. It seems terrible now to say that when I went to Central I still didn't know for sure that that was what I wanted to do.

Later on I got really told off by Walter for laughing. We did a performance of J.B. Priestley's *Time and the Conways,* and at one point I was hiding in a bay window. Richard Page-Jackson had to come and pull open the curtains so that I was discovered, and one night he pulled the curtain so hard that it came off the rail and the whole thing came down and hit me on the head. My next line was, 'I suppose you do that to all your girlfriends', and the audience howled, and I howled too. I was weeping with laughter, and I was rightly told off for it. Walter said I was highly unprofessional, it was a very naughty thing to do, and I was never, ever, ever to do that again. However, when I got to the Old Vic Walter Hudd was in the company, and I have never seen anyone laugh onstage like him. I was playing the Princess of France, wooed by Donald Houston as Henry V. Walter was the King of France, and he laughed his whole way through it. I thought, Oh my cup is full, it's come full circle.

At the end of our third year at Central we all had to do our final show at Wyndham's Theatre in the West End, with only about six people present from different theatre managements. I did Miranda's speech from *The Tempest:* 'Alas now! Pray you, work not so hard.' Julia Wootton was there for the Old Vic, and she must have gone back and said something, because Walter Hudd came to me and said, 'Judi, they want you to go and audition at the Old Vic.'

I thought they wanted me to walk on, and that was my dream come true. But I was terrified when I got there, because there were masses of people, and John Dexter was organising the auditions. He said, 'Oh, Judi, would you come forward please,' and I did Miranda's speech again. Then Michael Benthall, the Director of the Old Vic, came up and said, 'Will you go away and learn Ophelia's speech: "Oh, what a noble mind is here o'erthrown?" ' He kept asking me my height, so I really thought it was to walk on. I went back on a Saturday morning and did the speech, and Michael walked up on to the stage and said, 'I'm going to take an enormous risk, I'm going to cast you as Ophelia. If it's not working, I'll ask you to step down and you can understudy. I don't want you to tell anyone. OK?'

■ ■ ■ ■

2
THE OLD VIC
1957–1960

■ ■ ■ ■

When I returned to York for the Mystery Plays I had to obey Michael Benthall's instructions about keeping the Ophelia casting a secret until he was ready to announce it. So I just told everyone that I was going to the Old Vic, and people said, 'Oh wonderful, maybe one day you will be playing leading parts there.' I only told Mummy and Daddy and swore them to secrecy, and naturally they were both thrilled.

I arrived in 1957, the final year of the Old Vic's five-year-plan to perform all the plays of Shakespeare. *Hamlet* was the only play to be repeated. In the first year Richard Burton was Hamlet with Claire Bloom as his Ophelia. I was now to play her opposite John Neville, who had succeeded Burton as the leader of the company. Both men had brought new young audiences flocking to the Old Vic, because of their charisma and great acting talent. When I turned up on the first day for rehearsals I met Barbara Leigh-Hunt, Adrienne Hill and Juliet Cooke, and said, 'How do you do.' Everybody addressed each other as Mister or Miss, it was what you did then.

I took over a flat in Queen's Gate from Bill Johnson, who had been a year ahead of me at Central, when he left to go to another nicer one. I left for a much worse reason. The owners supplied sheets and laundry, but I developed an awful allergy to the washing powder they used. The day I arrived to do the nunnery scene in *Hamlet,* my left eye was completely closed up, and I was covered in spots. That night on the way home I went to St George's Hospital at Hyde Park Corner, and sat down by some people waiting. After I had been sitting there for about an hour and a half, someone said, 'What are you waiting for?'

'I'm waiting to see a doctor.'

She said, 'You don't have a number,' and sent me away.

I vowed I would never go in that place again ever, and I never have, even though now it has been converted into that very posh hotel, the Lanesborough.

Coral Browne, who was playing Gertrude, said, 'You're allergic to Michael Benthall!' She and her husband Philip Pearman had a lovely house on Chester Terrace in Regent's Park, and they moved me into the separate flat there on the top floor. We opened with *Hamlet* in Liverpool for a week to run it in — this was long before public previews — and when we got back to London, Barbara and Juliet asked me, 'Do you want to come and share No.9 Eaton Terrace with us, at £3 a week?' They had been sharing with Adrienne Hill, but she was moving somewhere else.

In my first year I was being paid £7.10s a week, which went up to £9 after I had been there a year. It was a wonderful flat, and we kept it scrubbed and clean, it was just like a new pin. I still think that was such a smart address, but there were moments when it didn't feel like it. One night coming home out of the Sloane Square tube station, I was walking by the pub on the corner past the Royal Court just as a man was being thrown out of it. He came flying into me, and we both ended up in the gutter. I thought, Well, that is pretty unfair.

The Liverpool reception for *Hamlet* was tremendous, I got notices the like of which I have never had since, saying things like 'The Vic takes a gamble, and a star is born'. John Barber, who was to become drama critic of the *Daily Telegraph,* came round and interviewed me. The press did make quite a thing of it prior to the London opening, so they were gunning for me after that. Richard Findlater was so outraged that he wrote in the *Sunday Dispatch:* 'How dare they use a completely unknown person . . . this is the equivalent of our National Theatre, how dare they do it.' Some years later Richard apologised handsomely to me, both personally and in print. But it did me a lot of good at the time. If you get bad notices for the first thing you do, it doesn't half bring you up with a jolt. I will have more to say about critics later.

I carried on and played the part for a year, and every single night I watched every play in the season from the wings. I don't think that is allowed any more, but I learnt so much from watching others. I was also playing First Fairy in *A Midsummer Night's Dream,* Juliet in *Measure for Measure,* Maria in *Twelfth Night* and I walked on in everything else, including *King Lear.* Paul Rogers was Lear, Coral Browne played Goneril, and Barbara Jefford was Regan. When the king entered, followed by his three daughters, they were followed by Barbara Leigh-Hunt, Adrienne Hill and me, with Barbara carrying a huge sword, Adrienne had a big tree, and I had an enormous smoking egg-cup, which excited not a little comment! One notice said: 'It was only too apparent who were the understudies, walking behind them all.'

I also walked on in *Henry VIII,* as well as understudying Anne Boleyn, when John Gielgud played Cardinal Wolsey to Harry Andrews's King, with Edith Evans as Queen Katharine. Sir John was so terribly funny; one night he came on with red spots all over his face, carrying a carnation, in the Cardinal's scarlet robe and biretta, and afterwards I heard somebody say, 'Sir John, that was a very puzzling make-up.' He said, 'Yes, well I suddenly read that he had a frightfully bad skin.' So we had this absolutely wonderful moment of dancing at Hampton Court, with Sir John in the middle, scarlet from head to foot, including his face.

It was from him that I learnt the beginnings of how to speak Shakespeare. I have always said to students that if you really want to know how to speak Shakespeare, Sir John and Frank Sinatra will teach you. Because one used to present the whole arc of a speech, and the other presented the whole arc of a song, without any intrusive extreme emphases. When I saw John Gielgud's one-man Shakespeare recital *Ages of Man* in New York I was absolutely bewitched by it. I didn't know him very well then, so I was a bit shy of going round, but I wanted to say thank you. About fifteen people were waiting to see him, but when he came out of his dressing room with somebody he suddenly saw me at the end of the queue and called out, 'Oh, please, Judi, do come in.' Then he turned to the rest of the queue and said, 'Judi and I were at the Old Vic together,' as if I had played leads with him instead of just walking on. There is nothing I would not have done for him then, or especially later when he restored my confidence at a very difficult time for me when I joined the Royal Shakespeare Company.

For *Henry V* I was wooed by three different actors playing the King. The most difficult time was when I was simultaneously playing the Princess of France opposite Robert Hardy in *The Age of Kings* on BBC TV in the daytime, and with Donald Houston at the Vic in the evening, with totally different costumes, totally different moves, and a few different cuts. After that, I could cope with Laurence Harvey taking over Henry when we went on the Old Vic's American tour, even though he never looked into my face, he just looked above my head; I felt nobody could be *that* tall!

The Old Vic was where I learnt how to be

part of a company, and John Neville showed me how a company should be led, which he did so brilliantly. When a lot of people caught Asian 'flu, we were so short of extras that on the line 'Let four captains bear Hamlet like a soldier from the stage' it was actually three girls and a rather old man struggling off with him. In *Henry VI* there was nobody left to play the Cade rebels except several girls. Then I got a bout of that 'flu as well, and went on to play Ophelia and cried the whole way through the performance. John really ticked me off afterwards. He said, 'Never ever, ever, ever do that again. That's not what they come to see you do. If you can't do it, let your understudy do it. What they come to see is the play and a story, and you having 'flu isn't part of it.' It is rather a harsh lesson to learn, but nevertheless it is no good saying, oh, my father has died or something, and I don't feel like it. That is not what the audience ever comes to see, they come to see that particular story and how you interpret it. So you have to learn to put those things in a little side-compartment sometimes, and draw on them when you need them.

In 1958 the company was about to embark on a six-month tour of America, and Michael Benthall sent for me. When I went in, he was standing, looking out of the window, and I think he found it quite difficult to break the news. He was a sweet and considerate man, with the best interests of his company always in his mind. He said, 'Judi, you didn't get very good notices as Ophelia. So when we go to America, you are not going to play her. How do you feel about it?' So I gulped a bit, and then he said, 'Do you still want to go?'

'I do, I do still want to go.'

'Well, you'll be out of *Hamlet* altogether, I wouldn't ask you to be in it. But I still want you to play the Princess of France, and Maria.' Both of those were very good parts. John Neville was waiting for me, because he knew what was coming, and I cried a great deal. Then I went and had all my hair cut off.

I must say it was quite hard not being in *Hamlet* when we got there. At the end of the tour it was to be televised in New York. I thought, What am I going to do? because by then I had seen most of the shows. So I put a notice up in the theatre saying: 'If anyone has any mending or things like that which they want doing before we go home, please leave it in my dressing room.' I got there the next day and I couldn't open the door: they had piled all their clothes up so that I just could not get in.

When we came back home, the company were asked to go to Yugoslavia with *Hamlet* and I got the part of Ophelia back. Michael asked me to his office and he said,

'Now, Miss Dench, I think you've learnt a lot in six months.'

'I hope so.'

'Well, I think you ought to play Ophelia in Yugoslavia.'

We played Belgrade, Zagreb and Ljubljana, and the audiences went absolutely mad. The students could not afford to come, so about six or seven of us went off to the university and did as much of the play as we could, just for them, for free. It was so exciting, I felt I played it better because I had watched Barbara play it in America, and I couldn't copy her performance because I am not like her, but I felt I understood it better.

If *Hamlet* had its difficult moments for me, then *Measure for Measure* was difficult for everybody. The American director Margaret Webster arrived at rehearsal with a broken leg in plaster, which only added to her famously bad temper. She certainly got off on the wrong foot with John Neville, who was playing Angelo. Barbara Jefford was Isabella, a part she had played at Stratford opposite John Gielgud, and on that very first day Margaret Webster turned to Barbara and asked her, 'I wonder what it was that made Sir John so wonderful as Angelo?' right in front of John.

At that time there was no Equity ruling about when a rehearsal had to stop, so whenever they were off everyone used to go to the wonderful old pub next door (now known as Bar Central). John used to lean against the door at half-past five, and when the door was opened he would fall on the floor and say, 'Sorry I'm late.' At the Technical Run there was a lot of stopping and starting, and at one point John came on to this vast timber set, well the worse for wear, struck a match and said, 'I name this ship *Disaster.*' Barry Kay was the designer, and Margaret Webster once gave him a terrible dressing-down. I felt so sorry for him; she screamed at him, and a lot of his costume designs were cut.

A Midsummer Night's Dream was much more fun, directed by Michael Benthall. To play Bottom, he cast the comedian Frankie Howerd, who was wary of the Shakespearean actors he was joining. He was lovely, and wonderful in the part, but he was a bit mean, and would never buy a drink for anybody, always managing to be the last one in the pub. All the actors playing the mechanicals very much stuck together, and had a dressing room upstairs whilst he was in Dressing Room One. Once when they were told to break for lunch they all came down and waited on the bend of the stairs until he came out. When he did, he glanced up and saw them, and along the corridor he suddenly stopped to do his shoelace up, so they all stopped as well. He said, 'What's wrong with you lot?' They said, 'We're waiting for you to tie your shoe and go in and buy us a drink at last.'

Another imaginative piece of Michael's off-beat casting was Tommy Steele as Tony Lumpkin in *She Stoops to Conquer.* I think the pop star was just as scared as the comedian of sharing a stage with classical actors, but his fans in the audience were quite restless until he came on. I still have the letter which one of them wrote to Tommy Steele during the run, which said:

Dear Mr Steele, My wife and I are coming to see She Stoops to Conquer *on Friday, and as it's my wife's birthday would you mind singing 'Little White Bull'?*

The stage doorkeeper, Ernie Davis, liked this letter so much that he asked Tommy for it, and now I have it.

Twelfth Night was also great fun to play,

51

especially with John Neville as Aguecheek, Derek Godfrey as Feste, and Paul Daneman as Sir Toby Belch. In the early rehearsals I began by playing Maria without an accent, and then one day Michael Benthall asked me if I could play it in anything else. I said, 'Yes, I could play it in Yorkshire', which I had heard often enough when I was growing up, and it seemed to fit the character very well. We had a lovely time doing it, and it is one of my favourite plays; I have done it twice more since then.

Michael Benthall was never really given the credit that was his due for his achievements at the Old Vic, nobody has written about him in the way he should have been written about. He was not perhaps the greatest director, but he had a wonderful eye as an impresario in choosing a company. In Richard Burton and John Neville he had the precursors of the Beatles and Johnnie Ray, the audiences used to go mad when they came on, and his courage in casting Frankie Howerd and Tommy Steele paid off at the box office. I owed Michael a lot, including the chance to play Juliet, which I am pretty sure he suggested to Franco Zeffirelli, to whom he gave his first opportunity to direct Shakespeare. John Stride was cast as Romeo, and Alec McCowen as Mercutio.

Nobody could remember when it had last been cast with actors so young: we were all in our early twenties.

Franco was quite unlike any other director I had ever worked for. I was used to them being down in the stalls, and asking you to make a certain move from out there. He rehearsed the scenes with Romeo and Juliet separately from the rest of the cast, and would tell us what to do, and you would be doing it, and suddenly he would be doing it beside you, which was a bit off-putting, because he was better than either of us. He put a fantastic passion into it, and the whole production had a hot Italian atmosphere about it, using dry ice to create what looked like a heat haze, people putting towels and sheets out over balconies, the boys lying asleep on the fountain — it looked absolutely beautiful. But Edith Evans didn't like it because, she said, we all looked so dirty.

I did not get very good notices for that, at least at first, and most of the critics hated it; only Kenneth Tynan raved about the production in the *Observer,* and I can still remember thinking, Bless him. We had all been dismayed by the overnight reviews, but Michael was like a rock. He called us all together, and told us to take no notice of critics without any vision. 'Go on, and listen to your hearts,' he said. So we did, and audiences flocked to it. We had the longest run of the play for ages — over 120 performances.

My parents came to everything I did at the Old Vic, and it was during this run that Daddy famously got so carried away when I cried out to Peggy Mount, 'Where are my father and my mother, Nurse?' that he called out from the stalls, 'Here we are, darling, in row H.' When I tell that story now, hardly anyone believes me, but I do assure you that it is true.

Then we took it to Venice as part of the Biennale, and played at the beautiful old Fenice Theatre, which years later sadly burnt down. We went up an hour and a half late, because of a gondola crush. Franco's relations came round in the interval and drank all the champagne; they had quite a party before they went off, leaving us to get on with the second part of the story. The curtain came down at a quarter past one in the morning, but it was a glorious experience, and those were the final performances I did of *Romeo and Juliet,* a pretty romantic place to play my last night with that production. The rest of the company went on to Turin, then toured at home before taking it to Broadway, but I didn't go with them because I was leaving the Old Vic to join the Royal Shakespeare Company. I thought that Franco would never forgive me for not going to America with it. Indeed, he was so angry that he wouldn't speak to me. I had to wait forty years before we worked together again.

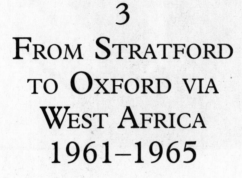

3
FROM STRATFORD
TO OXFORD VIA
WEST AFRICA
1961–1965

I joined the Royal Shakespeare Company for the first time in 1961 at the invitation of Peter Hall, who asked me to play Anya in *The Cherry Orchard.* It was to be directed by Michel Saint-Denis, and I had to go to meet Michel at Peter's house in that little square opposite Harrods. I remember that particularly, because Michel said, 'Oh, if I'd been looking for Eliza Doolittle my search would stop here,' so I don't think that I was his first choice as Anya. But nevertheless I did get the part. The cast included John Gielgud, Peggy Ashcroft, Patrick Wymark, Roy Dotrice, Dorothy Tutin, Patience Collier, Patsy Byrne and Ian Holm. It was the end of the Stratford season, which they had all been in, and I hadn't, so I did feel very much the new girl.

We rehearsed for eight weeks at Stratford, which was unusually long even at that time, before opening at the Aldwych, which had become the London base for the RSC. Not long after we started rehearsing, Peggy Ashcroft said to me, 'I have a feeling that you're going to have a hard time. Michel always picks on someone, just don't let him see you cry.' That was when my fondness for Dame Peg started, and for Sir John, too, who came to my rescue at a difficult moment. At the end of the first act Michel used to give notes to everybody, but when he got to me he would just shrug and throw up his hands and sigh, so my confidence, if I had any, just disappeared. Then one day when we were rehearsing in the Conference Hall, now the Swan Theatre, we reached the end of Act I, and Sir John said to me as we exited, 'Oh, if you'd been doing that for me in one of my productions, I'd have been delighted.' From that minute I was even more devoted to him. I thought, That's who I'll do it for, I'll just ever so slightly shift the emphasis, and do it for Sir John.

Apparently the first production of *The Cherry Orchard* that Michel had seen was by the Moscow Art Theatre, and he kept wanting me to do the same kind of tinkling laugh that the actress playing Anya there had done on her first entrance. He used to pretend that he didn't understand what I was saying, he kept going, 'What? What?' Once we had opened, and the production was a success, I suddenly became his flavour of the month, but it was ever so slightly too late for me by then, after eight weeks of rehearsal misery at Stratford.

I loved acting with Sir John, who got marvellous notices as Gaev, but somebody said on *The Critics* programme on the radio that he didn't feel Gaev was enjoying the caramels enough. So the next night he came on he was enjoying them so much that he completely dried on the line, and then laughed, of course. There is a story that may be apocryphal that somebody said to him in a play, 'I don't think you should wear the brown shoes, I think that the black shoes look better.' Somebody else said, 'I think the brown shoes are better,' so he wore one brown and one black shoe. I love that story.

While I was doing *The Cherry Orchard* at the Aldwych, Peter asked if I would like to go and do the 1962 season at Stratford, first to play Isabella in *Measure for Measure,* directed by John Blatchley, and then to be in *A Midsummer Night's Dream,* directed by himself, a revival of his original 1959 production, which I had seen with Mary Ure as Titania.

I enjoyed playing Isabella, with Ian Holm as my brother Claudio, Tom Fleming as the

Duke, and Ian Richardson as Lucio, though we only had mixed notices for it. But it was absolutely glorious to be in the *Dream*, playing Titania to Ian Richardson's Oberon, and Ian Holm's Puck. Lila de Nobili designed the most unbelievably exquisite set, which looked like an Elizabethan hall when you went in, and suddenly the lights came on and you saw a forest going right back, with Puck coming running through the trees. It was just magical. I thought then that Ian Richardson was simply the best Oberon there had ever been.

It was my idea for the fairies all to have those pointed rubber ears, and I had a brilliant wig that had been made in Paris out of yak hair, it was like the top of a dandelion. The clothes were Elizabethan and very mothy-looking; halfway down, my skirt became a cobweb. We were a bit dirty and all barefoot, which we covered with sparkly stuff, and Ian Richardson had to be told to use a bit less.

When we made the film of it at Compton Verney, Peter said that those costumes looked much too substantial and mortal in a real wood, so they started to get cut down, and cut down and cut down, and it ended up with me just being sprayed in green paint every morning. I kept the pointed ears, but was now given a very long wig, and they used to go out and pick tiny little ivy leaves, which just covered my modesty.

We were doing a pick-up shot one day, of me lying in the bower, and I had to lie in this special position because it was all marked out absolutely perfectly to match the previous shot. They said, 'We will be ready to go, but we must get all this exactly right,' so they were just putting leaves exactly where they were. I was very cold and still lying there, and then quite suddenly I had a worm on me — the only thing I am frightened of — so I leapt up and ruined the shot. Not only was I sprayed green, but I wore green Wellington boots all the time because of the worms.

At the same time as I was alternating Titania and Isabella on the Stratford stage, I was also commuting to London to play Dorcas Bellboys in *A Penny for a Song* at the Aldwych. I felt as if I was spending half my life driving up and down the A40. We worked on it with the author, John Whiting, and it is such a brilliant play, about a Dorset village in 1804 fearing a Napoleonic invasion, but the critics didn't like it at all. The others in the cast were Michael Gwynn, Marius Goring, James Bree, Newton Blick, Mark Eden and Gwen Ffrangcon-Davies, and we had a great time doing it. The Aldwych was a lovely theatre to play in, and much nicer than the Barbican, where the RSC moved later on. The dressing rooms there haven't got windows, it's not comforting, not attractive, you can't get supper afterwards. I felt it had nothing to do with the theatre, and I would never go there again to do a play. But we will come to the plays I did do there later on.

My contract with the RSC was coming to an end when I had a call from John Neville, inviting me to join his Nottingham Playhouse Company for their tour of West Africa. It was arranged by the British Council, and such a tour had never been done before; we went out there long before Peter Brook, who claimed to be the first some years later. The three plays were all the school set books — *Macbeth, Twelfth Night,* and Shaw's *Arms and the Man,* which I wasn't in. Before we left, John and I happened to meet Paul Rogers one day in Sloane Square; John had played Macduff to Paul's Macbeth at the Old Vic, and when Paul asked him what he was doing John told him, and then said this very endearing thing: 'I'm going to copy you.' I find too that after you have been in a play many times, the echo of how someone played the part is so strong when you come to play that part yourself. When I played Gertrude later I could only hear Coral Browne in the part, she was so wonderful.

In West Africa they had never seen a theatre company before, and had no idea what to expect. I played Viola in *Twelfth Night,* and the moment I met Sebastian at the end, when we did look very much alike, there was incredible excitement, it was almost a riot; in Lagos everybody threw programmes and rushed up to the stage. To bring the curtain down the stage manager had to phone a man called Mr Obeyme, who was looking through a hole in the back of the theatre, and say, 'Mr Obeyme — curtain — down.' It must have been an extraordinary system, but he was able to bring the curtain down. So we rehearsed that, and on the first night in Lagos, just before the curtain, he said, 'Mr Obeyme — curtain — down.' But he didn't bring the curtain down, after which he was called Mr Disobeyme.

That was the only real theatre we played in on the tour; elsewhere we were in the open air, often against huge curved cinema screens. Vultures would sit hunched at the top watching us, so during *Macbeth* I used to say, 'For goodness' sake twitch when you're killed, they're waiting to pick your bones.'

Every time I said, 'The Thane of Fife had a wife,' it used to bring the house down; anything that rhymed they found hysterically funny, and would call out, 'Say that again, say that again,' and then fall about. Any time we touched each other they absolutely howled with laughter, and they found the witches equally funny. When I went back with James Cairncross in 1969 on another British Council tour, this time just the two of us doing some recitals, we asked them why this was, and they said, 'Because it's very funny to see a white man believing in witches.' Nothing will ever throw you again when you have played to those audiences.

That first visit prompted a great surge of interest in theatre, with a whole lot of drama groups springing up all over the place. Everyone now seemed to be acting *Macbeth,* and in 1969 James and I saw it performed by young people several times. The most thrilling of all was a Lady Macbeth who laughed uncontrollably during it — it was really chilling. She may have been laughing entirely because she thought this was a very funny play about a white man believing in spirits, but nevertheless it was thrilling to watch.

In Ghana the company played for President Nkrumah, who was virtually a prisoner in his own palace; the security was fantastic, you couldn't even go to the loo without somebody accompanying you. At the university in Accra, I had not been feeling very well, and in the middle of *Twelfth Night* I completely fainted. Peter Blythe was playing Orsino, and he said, 'Ladies and gentlemen, I'm sorry, she's not very well,' and carried me off, to thunderous applause. They asked for a doctor, and he came and looked at me, and said, 'Undo her jacket please.' In order to play Viola disguised as Cesario I was wearing a roll-on to keep myself flat underneath the doublet, and he said, 'No wonder she's fallen down on the stage, it has the suspender belt round the wrong buttonhole.'

In fact I had caught malaria. The company were flying on to the next stop, and I was told not to travel on with them, but that idea did not appeal to me at all. I thought if I didn't I would be left there, so I went with them, and John and James virtually carried me on to the plane. I was feeling so ill that I don't remember much about it, but we had a four-day rest period, and in those four days I recovered, so I managed not to miss any performances. But poor Polly Adams had to once because of a terrible toothache from an impacted wisdom tooth, so I doubled that night as a witch as well as Lady Macbeth. I learnt later that I was not the first: Sybil Thorndike used to do that double regularly on her wartime tours.

During the tour we went to lunch with a man from the British Council, and in the middle of the lunch I suddenly had a premonition that was so strong I asked if I could phone home to England, in a total stranger's house. I rang home, and Daddy had just had his second heart attack. He had recovered from the first one in 1954, but this was much more serious, and somehow I sensed it thousands of miles away.

After that first West Africa tour, I had a very brief run in a disastrous play called *A Shot in the Dark* — a French play *L'Idiote* by Marcel Achard, translated into American idiom by Harry Kurnitz — and is barely worth mentioning except for the night it ground to a halt at the Lyric Theatre. The cast included Peter Sallis, Patricia Marmont and Polly Adams, and George Baker had to interrogate me. Polly had to enter and play a short scene as his wife, and then exit. This night we came to her entrance, and there was no Polly. Peter, George and I waited, and waited, and then we heard the stage manager go to the back and shout 'Polly'. There was still no sign of her, and we didn't know how to pick the scene up, so Peter said, 'I think I'll go and ask Monsieur Armand what he thinks about this,' and he walked off. We heard him rustling through the script trying to find my line, because the stage manager was now racing up the stairs trying to find Polly, and Peter came back to give me my cue, saying: 'Monsieur Armand suggests this . . .' So I said my line, and then George said to Peter, 'What do I say?' Peter said, 'If you think I'm going off to look up your line, you've got another think coming.' It was such a disaster, but thank goodness there was hardly anybody there. I hope it gave the audience a bit of a laugh, because they weren't having it in the rest of the play. Afterwards Polly said she thought she had already played the scene, and she was in the loo, knitting. This was my first experience of Peter's gift for improvisation, which came in useful much more often later on, when we were both in *Cabaret* together.

During this mercifully brief run my agent Julian Belfrage told me that Frank Hauser wanted me to join his company at the Oxford Playhouse to appear in Chekhov's

Three Sisters. I couldn't believe it, because on our only previous meeting I had thought he was so rude to me, and I was quite rude back. We each thought we had been snubbed by the other, and it was just a silly misunderstanding. I had also been told, quite wrongly, that he had walked out of *Romeo and Juliet* at the Old Vic. But now I became absolutely devoted to him, he was such a wonderful director. He was very intelligent, witty, funny, and precise. Tall and lean, he worked hard, and had such an insight into everything to do with the theatre. I once said that if Frank asked me to step in front of a bus, I'd do it. I'd know he had some good reason.

The Oxford Playhouse is a notoriously hard theatre to be heard in, especially under the circle. He used to do that most irritating thing, but of course the best possible thing: when you would say something like 'Pass me that book', Frank would shout, 'Pass me the what? Well, let me hear it then.'

He had a gift for casting, and that company included Joseph O'Conor, whom I had met in the York Mystery Plays, James Cairncross, with whom I had just worked, John Moffatt, who would also become a great friend, Roger Livesey, Elizabeth Sellars, John Standing and John Turner. Frank also had a keen eye for European plays that had never been seen in this country.

I had missed out on *Three Sisters* the year before, when Tyrone Guthrie had asked me to go and play Irina at his brand-new theatre in Minneapolis, but I had just signed the contract for the short-lived *A Shot in the Dark,* so I could not go. The Oxford production happened to be Frank's very first Chekhov, and it was a great success. I found John Turner a bit scary during rehearsals, because he used to send out for a quarter-pound of completely raw steak, into which he would mix an egg before eating it. I have to have my meat very well cooked, almost charred, so I found this very frightening. He was also incredibly tall, and in the next play, *The Twelfth Hour,* I had to kiss him passionately, so Frank had to devise a tree-stump for John to fall over, as there was no other way I could reach him to kiss him at all. This was a modern Russian play, and its author, Aleksei Arbuzov, came over to see us in rehearsal. Two years later he offered Frank his next play, *The Promise,* which was to prove very important to my career.

We did *The Alchemist* next, and Frank suggested that I cut my hair short to play Dol Common, donning a long wig when I was pretending to be the Queen of Faery, which

I tore off and stamped on at one point in the plot. My two fellow tricksters, Face and Subtle, were played by John Turner and Alan MacNaughtan.

It was during the rehearsals in London for *The Alchemist* that I had my second premonition. I had set off from my flat in Regent's Park Terrace when I suddenly had the strongest feeling that I should go back and ring Daddy. I talked to him and Mummy for about twenty minutes, and then set off again for the rehearsal, and now I was quite late, when usually I am one of the first to arrive. Daddy died later that day, just after midday. I didn't know he was going to die, it was the same as in West Africa, I just knew I had to talk to him.

After my brother Peter broke the news to me, I rang Frank Hauser, and he immediately guessed from my voice that something had happened. He said he would come straight over, and when he arrived he just said, 'I presume it's one of the family.' After the funeral in York he rang and invited me to bring Mummy back to Oxford with me, saying he would find her some work to do in the wardrobe department, he knew how good she was at that, and it was a great help to both of us at such a sad time.

We ended that Oxford season with two

French plays, the first by Anouilh, *Romeo and Jeannette,* in which the two lovers commit suicide at the end, just like Shakespeare's pair, but the modern play was much more difficult to get right. I had to have a lot of energy in the part, and I got a note from Frank Hauser one night, saying, 'When you come in through the door will you refrain from lifting the entire back-set off the floor?'

The second was *Le Chandelier* by Alfred de Musset, which had not been seen in England since 1910, and we performed it under the title *The Firescreen.* It was directed by Minos Volanakis, who was quite a livewire. He told me that I couldn't possibly go on playing under the name Dench. Minos thought the food we had to eat looked a bit dull, so he sent the stage manager out to get a huge bottle of maraschino cherries, who then tipped it into a tin of Irish stew, which we were suddenly confronted with on the first night. Simon Ward laughed so much he blew into his glass, and the contents went right up in the air; there was red wine dripping all over him, and then we had to play our love scene. The whole evening had got off to a bad start, as I had been out to lunch, come back and made up, gone onstage and climbed into the bed ready for the opening scene. The stage management glanced over to check that I was in bed and brought the curtain up, but by then I had nodded off. Frank Shelley was playing my husband, André, and he came on and said my name, 'Jacqueline', and I woke up startled and replied, 'Frank!'

I was wondering where to go next when I had the second call from John Neville to join him at the Nottingham Playhouse, but I only said au revoir to Oxford.

■ ■ ■ ■

4
EXCITING TIMES AT NOTTINGHAM AND OXFORD 1965–1967

■ ■ ■ ■

When John Neville invited me back to Nottingham in 1965 he offered me five very different plays over the two seasons. The first was Isabella again in *Measure for Measure,* but this time in a modern-dress production very unlike the Stratford one. I was dressed in a white shift that was vaguely nun-like, but Edward Woodward played Lucio in a white macintosh and dark glasses. He looked rather like the private investigator he played later in the long-running TV series *Callan.*

Lucio has a speech saying:

'Go to Lord Angelo,
And let him learn to know, when maidens
    sue,
Men give like gods; but when they weep
    and kneel,
All their petitions are as freely theirs
As they themselves would owe them.'

And Teddy Woodward just could not learn that speech, so on the first night he said instead: 'Go to Lord Angelo, and make him learn to know, that when maidens kneel down they can have anything they want,' and he handed me a cigarette through the bars. He improvised quite a lot, and missed out words. At the end, just before the disguised Duke reveals himself, Lucio had to say to him: 'O thou damnable fellow! Did not I pluck thee by the nose for thy speeches.' Teddy couldn't remember the word 'nose' so just said: 'Pluck thee about the speeches,' and I had to move upstage for a bit to recover.

I had a tricky moment when I had to enter the moated grange, which John Neville had turned into a nightclub. At the first rehearsal I asked him how I was supposed to come into such a club, and he said, 'The way any f****** nun comes into a nightclub after hours' — which was not a lot of help.

John persuaded me to join him in the Playhouse's poetry and jazz evenings with Johnny Southgate, which he had been doing there for ages, and said, 'You ought to have a go at them.' I was frightened at first, but I am very glad I did them. They were done late at night or on a Sunday, and the audience used to bring their drinks in with them. I seem to have done quite a lot of readings and recitals since then, with or without jazz accompaniment.

By now John was like an old style actor-manager, except that there was nothing old about him. He was terribly disciplined, and he just knew how to run a theatre, and the whole place was full all the time, people used to be absolutely crowding into that theatre. They came not just for the plays but for the restaurant and the exhibitions, or just to look at the photographs. There were so many things going on, and there weren't many theatres that did that in the Sixties. It isn't every actor who can become a wonderful director/producer like that, with the foresight to initiate things. He thought the theatre should be a place where people met and exchanged ideas, and had a whole community feeling about it. I don't remember ever seeing an empty seat at the Playhouse.

Playing in Noël Coward's *Private Lives* felt like going to a party every night, it was like a wonderful kind of love affair, it was the most tremendous fun. Teddy was playing Elyot, and as Amanda I had a beautiful dark red wig with marcelled waves; the first time I was made up and in costume he walked straight past me, he had no idea who I was.

On the first night, my bracelet flew off into the audience, the lid came off the coffee pot and Teddy picked it up and put it in his top pocket. He pushed me into the top of the trolley, I couldn't get out of it and he refused to help me. It was one of the most riotous first nights I remember. Not surprisingly, the audience didn't want to let us go. The row scene is quite tricky to play, because it is terribly precise, and really difficult to time it properly, but the director Ronald Magill was a great help in getting that right.

He also directed *The Country Wife*, which I did with Harold Innocent as my puritanical and jealous husband, and Michael Craig as the rake trying to seduce me. That was fun to play onstage, whereas most of the fun in Pauline Macaulay's *The Astrakhan Coat* was offstage. That was a dreadful play. Michael Craig got very, very drunk, and at one point when I opened the door to go out past a blackamoor figure standing in the corner holding a tray, instead of the blackamoor there was Michael blacked-up with a towel round him. I don't think anybody in the audience saw him, but I did, and that was a difficult moment.

Job Stewart and I played a trick of our own on Harold Innocent in *St Joan*, where he was playing the Inquisitor, and we thought he was over-milking every minute of his hugely long speech in the trial scene. So on the day of the opening we asked John Neville if we could do that scene in full as the warm-up beforehand. As Harold began his speech Job produced a flask from under his habit and poured out cups of tea for all the monks, Ronald Magill as Cauchon took out a long piece of knitting, and all the rest were doing crosswords, playing chess or cards. Harold was so mad at us, he stopped and said, 'Do you want me to go on with this, John?' by which time John was laughing so much he had to lie on the floor between the rows of seats.

My costume for Joan was knitted chain-mail. That was when I was really aware of the absurdity of it all, after we were delayed on Act II. I was standing in the Green Room and I looked out of the window and saw this woman pushing a pram, with two children and a whole lot of bags, and then I turned and looked at all this knitted chain-mail on everyone, and thought, Oh God, what are we doing?

I adored playing Joan, but I would play her very differently now. I would play her as a real troublemaker, a real pain in the arse, which she must have been. She must have been insufferable, and I am sure that that is the way to play her.

It was during the run of *St Joan* that the director Christopher Morahan came up to Nottingham to see it, and to bring me the script of John Hopkins's TV quartet *Talking to a Stranger,* to ask me to consider the part of Terry. John was one of the main writers for the pioneering police drama series *Z-Cars,* and I had played the part of the brittle young girl — Terry in embryo — in an episode of that series, but when I read these scripts I thought, I can't do this, I really can't. I said to John that there were so many things I wouldn't understand; that girl was such a complex character, how would I manage? He said he would sit outside the rehearsal room in the car, so that I could go and ask him.

Maurice Denham and Margery Mason played my parents, and Michael Bryant was my brother, and each of the four episodes was seen from the perspective of each of us in turn. Terry was a very highly strung character, in a panic about being pregnant and how to tell her family, and the whole thing was emotionally very taxing. It helped that her flatmate Jess was played by Pinkie Johnstone, who became one of my closest friends, but we were still both reduced to tears at some rehearsals. Maurice was not unlike my own father, and the four of us did really become very much like a family over the weeks of rehearsal and recording. My attitude to Maurice and Margery and Michael will never alter; I did feel we all went through something together, though sadly all three of them are now gone.

One day in the pub Michael said that he was feeling a bit drowsy, and I said flippantly, 'Well, if I was the director I'd give you the afternoon off.' Christopher Morahan hit the ceiling, he was under terrible strain at the time, because I think his wife was very ill. Nobody spoke, so then Maurice put his hand on my knee under the table, which made it worse, of course. I got my money out, and I just put it down for my lunch, and got up and left the pub. As I left the pub in Shepherd's Bush there was the most unbelievable screech of brakes as a car hit a jeep, and John Hopkins came racing out after me. He and I walked around until the end of lunch, and I believe Michael Bryant spoke his mind to Christopher. Then we went back for notes, and I smoked a whole packet of cigarettes — and I don't smoke.

Christopher is a marvellous director, and what was so brilliant about John as a writer was that this was the first time on television when people overlapped their lines, and talked across each other like they do in real life. *Talking to a Stranger* got tremendous notices, and we all received an incredible amount of mail after it went out. It wasn't totally autobiographical, although John had in fact drawn on real people and incidents in his own family, but one of them rang him afterwards and had not recognised it to be about themselves.

I won my first BAFTA Best Actress Award for playing Terry; I had really done very little television before this, and certainly nothing so demanding emotionally, so that made it even more special. My busy years in television were still some way off.

For now I returned to Oxford, because I was devoted to Frank Hauser and hugely admired him as a director. He had such great successes with those rarely performed or unknown European plays. The first one I did this time was Pirandello's *The Rules of the Game,* with Leonard Rossiter, directed by James Grout. Leonard and I didn't quite hit it off to begin with; he worked everything out in advance, whilst I tend to develop a part in the rehearsal room, but then we clicked, and the production had some very good notices. I was given some beautiful

Twenties costumes as Silia, which made me look a little like Sophia Loren.

As soon as we opened in that play, we began rehearsals for the next — *The Promise* by Aleksei Arbuzov. I have since been told that Frank was convinced that the part of Lika was written specially for me, after Arbuzov saw me in his earlier play *The Twelfth Hour*, but neither of them told me that at the time. True or not, it was a most rewarding, if exhausting part. The two men in my life were played by Ian McKellen and Ian McShane, and the three of us meet first at the Siege of Leningrad in 1942. Act II is in 1946, when Lika has to choose which of them to marry, and makes the wrong choice. In Act III we meet again in 1959 to try and correct that mistake. It was over three hours long, with a lot of ageing to do, and several costume changes, which kept us all busy. I used to go to sleep all the time during Frank's notes. There was a big bed I used to lie on, and Frank would say, 'Is she awake? Is the pussy awake? Because I have a few notes.'

Trevor Nunn had succeeded Peter Hall at the RSC, and he came to see me before the press night in Oxford, to ask me to go to Stratford the following year to play Kate in *The Taming of the Shrew,* and he had already cast Michael Williams as Petruchio. I said, 'Oh, that's a brilliant idea. But by the way, if *The Promise* is a success I have to go with it to London.' This was after the matinee performance and Trevor said, 'Well, it's absolutely charming,' but neither of us thought it would transfer.

Then we had the most extraordinary first night I can remember. None of us had anybody at it that we knew, not Frank, nor either of the Ians, nor me, because otherwise what followed could not have happened. The four of us decided that afterwards we would all go to a little Italian downstairs restaurant just round the corner from the Randolph Hotel, and only a stone's throw from the theatre. When we walked in, there was a huge table in the other half of the restaurant, taken up with every single critic. So we rather sheepishly looked at them, and they looked at us, and looked away, and then they all said, 'Will you come and join us for coffee?' So we went and sat with them, and they were all so extraordinarily complimentary. We didn't have to avoid talking about the play, because all they wanted to talk about was the play. That was when we thought, We are in here with a winner — which it was. I don't ever remember such a thing happening before or since.

We transferred to the tiny Fortune Theatre in Covent Garden, and it was even harder work up all those stairs to the dressing rooms. As we came down from the matinee, we only had about half an hour to transform ourselves back into the wartime teenagers for the evening curtain-up. There was hardly time to put our feet up and have a cup of tea.

At the opening of the third act, when I entered with Ian McKellen as my husband, we were in fur hats and coats, and there was a very long time while we came in and took the coats off, neither of us spoke for several minutes, we just went in and out not speaking to each other; it said a lot about the marriage. One night we heard this woman remark absolutely clearly, 'Oh, all them furs, anyone would think they were in Russia.'

Another night I had a letter in the second interval from a friend of ours in York, a charming elderly lady called Mrs Bytheway. I said to Ian McKellen, 'She says in this letter that she is a huge fan of yours, and is coming round to see me, so please come round to my dressing room to meet her.' Ian asked, 'What's her name?' 'Mrs Bytheway.' 'What a strange name.' We went on for the third act, and what we hadn't realised was that the very first line of the third

act began, 'By the way . . .' We were speech-
less for a moment.

We heard that Richard Chamberlain was
coming one night. He was still playing Dr
Kildare on TV at that time, and Ian Mc-
Kellen became very excited. I used to have
the first dressing room, and his was on the
floor above, so he said, 'If he comes round,
you've got to tap on that water pipe in the
corner, and then I'll come down and just
drop in as I'm passing.' So I said, 'OK, if he
does come round,' and after the performance there was indeed a knock on the
door, and Richard Chamberlain came in. I
said, 'How absolutely wonderful to see you,
do come in, please.' The dressing rooms
were tiny, and the only place he could possibly stand was in the corner against the
pipe that I was meant to be tapping for Ian
McKellen. I thought, How do I edge up to
him? Can I put my arm around him in order
to tap on it with something like a penny, or
a stick of make-up or something in my
hand? How on earth can I do that? So I
couldn't, of course, and then Ian eventually
dropped in anyway, about twenty minutes
after the curtain came down, and said, 'Oh,
do you have any cotton wool? Oh, good gra-
cious, look who's here — Richard
Chamberlain.'

An even more important visitor, from my point of view, was Hal Prince, who came to see it, and rang my agent the next day to say he wanted to see me about playing Sally Bowles in his forthcoming production of *Cabaret.* I thought it was a joke, but Julian said he was quite serious. He took me out to lunch first, before I went to the audition, and I had a glass of wine, because I was absolutely petrified when I went into the theatre and had to sing for Hal. I said, 'If you don't mind, I think I'll sing it from the wings.' It was my first musical, and I was amazed to get the part, but I learnt an awful lot from doing it, especially from Hal, who must be one of the best directors of musicals ever.

■ ■ ■ ■

5
CABARET AND
RETURN TO THE
RSC
1968–1970

■ ■ ■ ■

I am a great believer in seeing whatever is playing at the theatre you are about to act in, because then you get the measure of everything; I know that is why I got into the Old Vic. So when I was given the part of Sally Bowles in *Cabaret,* James Cairncross said, 'Right, we'll go to see *The Desert Song* at the Palace.' All I remember of the actual show is that there was one man in the chorus who was very under-made-up; all the Arabs were a dark brown colour except him; James and I laughed and laughed.

I was very apprehensive about the songs, because I am not a singer. But Hal Prince told me to go and read Christopher Isherwood's original novel, *Goodbye to Berlin.* 'Just read about her, and you will read that Sally was an English girl, Cheltenhambred, and she can't sing, but there was something about her that meant Cliff simply couldn't stop watching her. She would never make it as a singer, couldn't possibly be a success, but there was something charismatic about her.'

So I read about that, and then when the musical director was going back to New York during the rehearsals he asked me, 'Is there anything you want me to bring you?' I said, 'I want you to bring me the last note of *Cabaret* please.' Hal overheard that, and he said, 'If you can't get it, act that you can't get it.' It was such a wonderful director's note. I know that people who do musicals know that note, but I didn't. The other thing I learnt from Hal was that the story doesn't stop for the song; it is just carrying on part of the story, and if it doesn't it shouldn't be in there anyway. There should be no discernible line between the speaking, going into the song, and then coming out of it. That was such a wonderful piece of advice, and thank goodness he had just great faith in the fact that I would be able to do it.

He had produced many successful musicals, and when we rehearsed the Sailors' Dance there was a moment when I jumped and they all caught me, but Hal said, 'Oh no, cut that musical crap, everybody does that, don't do that.' He had very fresh ideas about everything, and he was great fun. Towards the end of rehearsals, he said, 'Just break out of it now, break out and do what you feel you want to do.'

It was a very happy company, and I used to leave my door open all the time for everybody to drop in and give me notes and tips. The girls used to make those glorious eyelashes out of black paper, very thin and marvellously cut, and they used to give me theirs. Sally Bowles had to wear green nail varnish, and you couldn't get it here then, so it had to be sent over from America.

I had a bit of a problem with Lila Kedrova who was playing Fraulein Schneider to begin with, because she had the dressing room next to mine and I think she got a bit unnerved by all these people coming into my room all of the time. She seemed to think that we were all ganging up against her, so I just walked into her room and said, 'Lila, what is this?' She pretended that she didn't know what I meant, but after that we were quite friends, though not friends like I was with Thelma Ruby, who followed her in the part, and helped me find things for my new house.

That was the idea of my friend Theo Cowan, the publicist, who rang up and said, 'I've seen a house you should buy.' 'Theo! Buy a house?' I had no intention of buying a house, but he insisted, 'Yes, of course you can do it.' It was in Prospect Place, overlooking the churchyard of Hampstead Parish Church, and the price was £14,400. That seemed a huge amount of money to me, but I was so glad that I bought it, which proved to be a brilliant move, and I owed it all to Theo. We went up to see it with Marty Feldman, the comedian. I cannot imagine what the owner thought watching us arrive — great big tall Theo, Marty with his bulging eyes, and this dwarf beside them. After I bought it, Thelma and I used to go down to Brighton, have breakfast on the Brighton Belle, and go looking for furniture.

My dressing room at the Palace was in the basement, so I could hear the comments of people passing by. There were three that I still treasure:

'Judi Dench in *Cabaret*! No one will go to see that, dear — no one!'

'Arthur, you told me it was all about nuns and children!'

'Well, where was Frankie Vaughan? I was waiting for Frankie to come on and sing "Come to the cabaret"!'

I was more concerned about the scenery sticking during the show. It was a complicated set, with a lot of sliders that came in, and they often got stuck. I seem to have had a lifetime of scenery getting stuck.

Sometimes we used to just come on and play the scene without it and improvise on a bare stage. That was wildly exciting, just making it up as we went along, though it could be tricky, especially in the last scene, where Sally had to tell Cliff that she has had the abortion. Peter Sallis was the Jewish greengrocer, and he was brilliant at just going on and chatting to the audience whilst the stage crew wrestled with the scenery.

The show had a mixed reception from the critics, but the audiences loved it, and it looked set for a long run. I said I would only do it for nine months, and Elizabeth Seal was going to take over my part. She was a huge star after *Irma la Douce,* and there was no sign of bookings falling off, but then Emile Littler, who owned the Palace Theatre, did the dirty on us. They had arranged a last-night party for me, which turned out to be the last-night party for everyone, because Emile wanted to bring in other shows. He brought in three of them in rapid succession, including the comedy *Mr and Mrs* with John Neville and Honor Blackman, and they all folded. I thought, Serve him right, that will teach him to laugh in church.

Towards the end of the run of *Cabaret* Trevor Nunn came to see me, and asked me for the second time if I would go back to Stratford and do *The Winter's Tale* and other plays during the season. I had long wanted to work with Trevor, but now he asked me to play Hermione, the mother of Perdita, and I was rather shocked that it was to be a maternal part. I wrote him a card, saying, 'Is it mothers' parts already?' Then a few weeks later he asked me if I would consider doubling the parts of Hermione and Perdita, which had not been done since Mary Anderson did it at the Lyceum with Forbes Robertson back in 1887. (By a curious coincidence, she had been married in the same church as I was, but I am getting slightly ahead of myself.)

I thought that to play such a double would be fantastically exciting, and so it was, in a most beautiful production, set in a great white box. Barrie Ingham played my husband Leontes, and Richard Pasco was Polixenes. To begin with, I was not totally convinced that the doubling would work onstage, but Trevor was so sure about it that I trusted his judgement, and the statue of Hermione coming alive at the end brought gasps of surprise and disbelief every night.

We played it in modern dress, and at an early rehearsal Trevor devised a marvellous exercise in setting up the King's jealousy.

Barrie, Richard and I were lying on a beach with me between the two of them, and of course if you are lying on your front on a beach your head naturally goes to one side when you are sunbathing. So this was all set up, and then Barrie got up and did a kind of swim right round the outside of the room. We just laughed a huge amount, that is the thing that keeps you sane; it does for me at any rate, I can't speak for everyone. Unless you can afford to make terrible jokes at your own expense, and laugh at yourself, I just don't think you can begin. I think you have got to be prepared to make such ghastly mistakes; sometimes you make them onstage at the expense of the audience, you don't mean to but you just think, Oh, I'll try this and give it a whirl.

The next play was *Women Beware Women,* directed by Terry Hands. He was a wonderful director, and later took over the running of the RSC; now he runs Theatr Clwyd in Wales. I liked working with Terry, and it was a marvellous production, but I don't feel I have ever been able to serve Terry up with the right performance. Middleton's text was fiendishly difficult to learn, and the final technical run went on until three in the morning. After it Brewster Mason, who was playing the Duke of Florence, produced a bottle of champagne, the only drink I really like, and we went off to drink it in the moonlight. We were certainly ready for it by then.

The food for the banquet was brought in from a place called Pargeter's in Bridge Street in Stratford. I remember there was a lot of chicken in breadcrumbs. At this stage I had been seduced by the Duke, I had no lines to say, and I could behave quite badly. I used to think to myself, Am I going out to dinner tonight? No, nobody's here that I know. So sometimes when Elizabeth Spriggs as Livia was speaking I would get up and lean right across, take her chicken leg off her plate and eat it. I had the most incredible time, just tucking into everything.

That play was nowhere near as popular with audiences as *Twelfth Night,* which followed it. This was my second time as Viola, whom I first played on the West African tour. John Barton, the director, was rather like a teddy bear with a big beard, and he had some disconcerting habits. He would perch on the back of a chair and chew razor blades, and used to drink pints of milk out of a beer-tankard. The whole stage was wood-slatted, with great candles on both sides, and on the very first night he got up to give notes to Lisa Harrow and to me, tripped on the top step and threw a whole pint of milk all over the stage. This was actually one of the few occasions when he gave me any notes; he hardly gave me any normally, and I was very unhappy about that.

Donald Sinden was quite brilliant as Malvolio, and he invented a wonderful moment on one entrance. He was just about to speak his first line when he looked at the sundial, looked up at the sun, then he took out his watch, looked at his watch, looked back at the sundial, put his watch back, and then moved the sundial round. It used to bring the house down.

Roger Rees played Curio, and he is another great joker. He found a pack of cards with animal pictures that the children used to play with in the Green Room, and he invented this really terrible game, where you had to have a card about your costume which you flashed in the last scene without the audience seeing. He called it 'Rabbit in the ruff' but it also became known as 'Badger in the boot' or 'Ferret in the foot'. It was very exciting, and it didn't half get you through that interminable last scene. I am afraid that at one performance I was unable to resist the temptation to reword Viola's line to Olivia about her virginity: 'Nor never none shall be mistress of it' to 'Nor Trevor

Nunn shall be mistress of it'. I don't think he has ever quite forgiven me for that Shakespearean sacrilege.

At the end of 1969 *Twelfth Night* was one of the plays the RSC took on tour to Japan and Australia. We were given an advance warning: 'Now you won't get any laughs in Japan,' which is quite a burdensome thing to carry on with you when you are about to do that play. I was glad somebody warned us, because it was very difficult to gauge how it was going. If you have had an enormous laugh on a particular line for ages, then suddenly you say the line and there is no laugh at all, that makes you completely lose it, because you leave the pause, and there is nothing to fill it. But then at the end they just went mad with applause.

We may have communicated to the audience, but it was a different matter with the stage crew, very few of whom understood any English. This became apparent during rehearsals for *The Winter's Tale* on Hermione's first walk across the stage. Our stage manager asked the Japanese interpreter to instruct the follow-spot operator at the back of the gallery, 'Tell him that when Miss Dench appears he has to follow her.' When I entered, the spotlight came on, but when I moved it failed to move with me. We kept redoing the walk, with a lot of accompanying shouting in Japanese, but the follow-spot never moved. Finally it was explained that 'a denchi' is Japanese for a torch battery, and he was waiting for a torch battery to come on.

I was not in the third play we took, *The Merry Wives of Windsor,* so I took the opportunity to go and see the *Noh* plays and the *Kabuki* theatre. We were taken into the *Kabuki* and allowed to watch them making up, but nobody spoke at all. All the actors sat on the floor, with a little marked area around them, making up very quietly with a mirror. Then suddenly, as we stood there, a young man came along and knelt down and said something in Japanese, so we were riveted to this man making up, who was very short and stout and wearing glasses. All this went on for a very long time, and when we went out into the corridor we asked what the young man had been saying. We were told, 'That is a young actor in the cast, coming up and kneeling to say to the star, "I am not worthy to act with you." ' A sentiment quite unheard of at the RSC!

Then we went into the theatre for the performance, and saw the *hana-michi,* the Seven Great Steps to Heaven from the stage, that long platform that goes all the way to the back of the auditorium. We were sitting right next to it when suddenly this exquisite figure walked along it very slowly dressed in white, and we realised that this was not a woman but the little plump man with the glasses we had watched making up backstage. It was a total transformation of a person, and absolutely breathtaking.

After Japan we took *Twelfth Night* to Australia, where the audiences were a bit noisier during the performances, not just at the end. This was the scene of a major change in my personal life, which might have happened earlier if I had gone back to the RSC in 1967 instead of 1969, and played Kate to Michael Williams's Petruchio then. We had actually known each other since 1961, when I was playing Juliet at the Old Vic and he was in David Storey's play *Celebration* at the Duchess Theatre. One night I was going to a play with Raymond Mander and Joe Mitchenson, the theatre historians, who took me under their wing and took me to see everything that was on in the theatre. When I was at Central we used to go to the theatre all the time, we all used to be in the gallery slips, and you could get into the Old Vic for sixpence. But when Ray and Joe took me we would sit in proper seats. They knew about everybody in the theatre, and were fantastically good friends to me.

This particular night we went for a drink in the pub Sweet Nell of Old Drury, close to the Duchess, and Michael was in the bar, and that was how we met. I thought, What a wonderful looking boy — which he was. We had a hugely good laugh, and that was it. I used to see him occasionally; I remember us once having tea in Covent Garden, when we sat rather vacantly, looking past each other. He came to the first night of *The Promise*, popped his head round the door and just said, 'Hello, terrific, terrific,' and was then off up the stairs to see the others. I knew him for nine years before we were married.

He was now in the other half of the company, playing Troilus in *Troilus and Cressida* at the Aldwych, and I was at Stratford. He damaged his kneecap playing football for the RSC, and had to have a cartilage operation which meant he was on crutches and couldn't go on for several weeks. In order to recuperate he came up to Stratford, where he had kept on his cottage at Armscote. One night during his convalescence Michael came to see *Twelfth Night* at Stratford, and joined us all for a drink at the Dirty Duck afterwards. We started to see each other quite often, but then we all went off to the Far East, and he went back for the last weeks of the run of *Troilus*. When that ended he decided, on the spur of the moment he always said, to fly out to Australia and surprise me. He certainly succeeded in that.

He knew many people in the company, and he had heard that we were all in a bad way because the actor playing Orsino in *Twelfth Night,* Charles Thomas, had died suddenly. Michael supposedly flew out just for one week, at the end of which we all said goodbye to him, and off he went to the airport. When we came back there he was in the bar again. Don Henderson walked in, saw Michael and went back out to look up at the sign, came back in and said, 'I thought it was The Duck we were in!' This happened every week for about six weeks.

Then Michael proposed, on a very beautiful day in Adelaide, but I said, 'This is absolutely no good at all. We had better wait for a rainy day in Battersea.' Because this was in Australia, we were on tour with the company, with glorious weather and swimming, and being fêted by people all the time. So the conditions were too wonderful to say yes — better to wait. Then he did propose again, back in England, not quite in Battersea, as it was in his flat in Kensington, but it was raining; and I hadn't seriously said no the first time.

We got married on 5 February 1971, in Hampstead's Catholic church just round the corner from my house in Prospect Place. My eldest brother, Peter, gave me away, and the ushers were Ian Richardson and Alec McCowen. Danny La Rue sat with his wedding present of two exquisite crystal glasses on his knee throughout the ceremony. There were more than 250 guests crammed into that little church, and the critic John Trewin and his wife enclosed a picture of Mary Anderson with their wedding present, to tell me that she had been married there (that was when I learnt that she had been the first to double Hermione and Perdita in *The Winter's Tale*). Then we all went off to the reception at London Zoo, which I had always liked since the days I had a flat near there.

Trevor Nunn had given us a lovely advance wedding present by casting Michael and me in his next production for the RSC at the Aldwych, Dion Boucicault's *London Assurance*. Trevor had come to meet the company at the airport when we returned from Australia, and saw Michael and me coming off together, which is why he cast us as the young lovers. The play had been unjustly neglected for years, and we all enjoyed ourselves hugely. Ronald Eyre directed it, and he sent me a note beforehand, saying, 'Do remember that Grace Harkaway is the sort of girl who would send valentines to herself, then fall over with the joy of it when the card arrived from herself.' That was a good note.

Michael was the young man who wins my hand, and Donald Sinden played his father, Sir Harcourt Courtly, as an elderly roué, heavily made-up like the outrageously camp actor Michael MacLiammoir. I had a long speech to Donald that got murmurs of laughter, turning to a kind of expectant buzz, and then an enormous burst of laughter. I used not to look at Donald too much during it, because Grace was off on a great flight of fancy, and I thought it was so wonderful the way the speech was going. It was only later that I glanced at Donald and saw that, as my speech got more flowery and more over the top, he very gradually looked out towards the audience, and pursed his red lipsticked mouth, with his eyebrow going up and down. It used to bring the house down, and I realised it wasn't my speech at all, it was Donald's reaction.

The production was such a hit that it ran

for two seasons. It was huge fun, we got great belters of laughs from it, the audiences loved it — apart from the broadcaster Alistair Cooke, who left before the end. But the grimmest audience was the night the Queen came with Edward Heath, then Prime Minister. It wasn't her fault, it was just that every time there was a line saying, 'Oh, the Queen's gone mad again', everyone looked at her for a reaction.

All the family were in this production; in addition to Michael and myself there was my brother Jeff and, for six months, my daughter Finty, as I was pregnant for most of the run. I had a lovely friend in Nottingham called Brian Smedley, who was a judge, and he had asked me to marry him. I had told him, 'I'll have to think about it, Brian.' But I never got in touch with him, and the next time I saw him I was about five months pregnant. He just put his head round the door of my dressing room and said, 'I take it the answer's no?' I was six months pregnant when I left the production in the last week. In the first scene Janet Whiteside had to say to me, 'Do you feel nothing stirring?' That got the biggest laugh.

After the last performance the cast gave me a huge Paddington Bear as a leaving gift for the baby; Grace Kelly was in the audi-

ence that night and Donald Sinden asked
her to present it to me.

■ ■ ■ ■

6
HAPPY FAMILIES
1970–1975

■ ■ ■ ■

The popularity of *London Assurance* ensured that it stayed in the RSC repertoire for longer than most productions. During this time I also did four markedly different plays. The first of these was *Major Barbara,* directed by Clifford Williams, who specialised in plays by Bernard Shaw. I had played Barbara on television eight years earlier, with Brewster Mason as Undershaft, and luckily he was also playing the same part again. He was a boyfriend of mine for a short while, and he used to take me to a little club near the Comedy Theatre, where I met several members of the Crazy Gang — Jimmy Nervo and Teddy Knox, and Monsewer Eddie Gray — and we all used to play the bluffer's game Spoof; that was good fun. In addition to Brewster, the cast included old friends Richard Pasco, Roger Rees and Elizabeth Spriggs.

The Merchant of Venice was much less fun.

I loathe the play, I think it is terrible, everyone behaves so frightfully badly. Who cares about anybody in it? My instinct was to say no when Trevor asked me, but then he talked me into it. Terry Hands was directing, and I think I drove him mad, but I couldn't do it, I never want to see it again, I wouldn't cross the road to see it, it is the only play of Shakespeare's I really dislike. Emrys James was playing Shylock, and there was rather an antagonism between us. Terry got very cross with me when we were rehearsing the scene with the knife. Antonio bared his chest and Shylock raised the knife, and I had to say, 'Tarry, Jew.' Whenever I said it, Terry would tell me, 'Don't say it yet.'

I had to wait until his hand was actually coming down to Antonio's chest, and I thought that was false. At one point Terry sent everyone else out of the rehearsal room and jumped up on to a table, he was so cross; I will never forget it. He said, 'You're not to be unkind to Emrys, his father was a miner.' I wasn't being unkind, I was trying to make sense of the scene. She would never have left it that long, she would have died of fright. How could she leave it until the knife was actually coming down on him? In one of the notices I was criticised for being self-indulgent, waiting for that moment.

Nothing went right. I had this idea of a wig for Portia with lots of curls, and John Neville came one night, I had not seen him for years, and he knocked at my dressing room, put his head round the door and just said, 'Hello, Bubbles,' that was all he said, and quite right too. But the worst moment happened onstage. Michael was playing Bassanio, and I had a speech to him in the Caskets scene:

'I speak too long; but 'tis to peize the
    time,
To eke it, and to draw it out in length,
To stay you from election.'

One night I said instead: '. . . to stay you from erection.' Well, the Wind Band stopped playing and left the stage, my brother Jeffery with Bernard Lloyd and Peter Geddis all left — nobody could stay. And I laughed. Poor Michael had a speech coming up, I have never seen him use his hands so much, and turn his back to the audience; it was terrible.

Michael and I played brother and sister in *The Duchess of Malfi;* he was Duke Ferdinand and I was the doomed Duchess. It is a difficult play, but I loved it. I kept thinking of that famous picture of Peggy Ashcroft as the Duchess eating the apricots, and it was thrilling to play. It was, though, very difficult to learn, and in fact I can't remember a single line from it, which is unusual for me. Clifford Williams was in charge of the production again and he made the most of it, though the notices were mixed for all of us.

By complete contrast, the Christmas play for children was *Toad of Toad Hall,* in which I played three parts — Mother Rabbit, First Fieldmouse and a Brave Stoat. Michael was Mole, Jeffery was Rat, Peter Woodthorpe was Toad, and Tony Church was Badger. So many of the children wanted to come round to see us, and I remembered my disappointment as a child when I did that. My family were all great fans of Gilbert and Sullivan, and when the touring company came to York two of the cast would always stay in our house. The girls said I had to go round afterwards, and I didn't know what that meant. The man who played Nanky Poo had a lovely voice, and a wonderful shock of black hair. When I went round they knocked on his door and said, 'Here's somebody who would like to meet you.' I walked in and saw this man who was bald; he had taken off his wig and was sitting there in a white vest with braces. So to avoid that kind of disappointment we made a plan at Stratford that we would not get out of our costumes, and just stay dressed as we were. But some of the younger children found it quite frightening to see someone in make-up for a badger or the other animals close up.

I got very sick during the run, with awful bilious attacks, and when the doctor came to see me I was being sick into a great big dustbin, still dressed as the Stoat. That was when I discovered my condition, because he said, 'Your trouble is you're pregnant.' I was already playing Mother Rabbit as very pregnant with lots of children, and now I really was.

Michael and I both thought the baby was going to be a boy, and decided on the name Finn. On 24 September 1972 I gave birth to a girl, and we called her Finty. She was actually christened Tara Cressida Frances, but has always been known as Finty to us and everyone else. We didn't think for a moment that she would be an actress. She wanted to be an acrobatic nurse, and I encouraged her, she would swing down the ward and take your temperature hanging upside down.

I wanted to give up working, to see that she was safely in the nest, but Michael said,

'Please don't.' So I tried to arrange it that in the beginning I was with her during the day, and going to the theatre in the evening when she was in bed. Then when she went to school later on I could do things like television during the day, to be with her in the evenings. To a large extent that was how it worked out. But I did do the BBC film of John Osborne's *Luther* not long after she was born, and I laughed the whole way through it, as all my nerve ends had gone to pieces after the birth.

My return to the stage was far from auspicious, and Michael and I only did it really because it was in York, at the Theatre Royal. The director, Richard Digby Day, had tried before to get us to go there, but the play he chose was *Content to Whisper,* adapted by Alan Melville from a French stage adaptation of a novel, *La Lumière Noire.* It has to be the most terrible play known to man, and very soon Richard knew it too. Sydney Tafler was the worst laugher with whom I have ever shared a stage. Sometimes it was so dreadful he just could not get the words out.

The only good thing about that return to York was being with Mummy and the rest of the family. She and Michael's parents hit it off immediately, and the three of them used to come and stay with us at Christmas and Easter. One night Michael said to me, 'Wouldn't it be wonderful if we could all just live together?' That was absolutely my idea of heaven, it is like a proper Quaker community, certainly for bringing up a child, but also the whole idea of looking after your parents. What appals me more than anything else in this country is just sending them off somewhere, where they sit like zombies in a room and they are just there to die. That is not to demean what the staff do in those homes, but I don't think it is healthy for the inmates.

We eventually found a converted stable block with eleven rooms just outside Stratford at Charlecote. Mummy moved in at the beginning of 1974, and Michael's parents, Len and Elizabeth, a little later. Finty remembers it so well, being brought up with her grandparents. It was not a very pretty building at all, it had been converted from some old stables into a modern L-shaped house with stone steps up to the front door, and it could actually have been converted very beautifully. It had three double bedrooms, all with their own bathrooms, a couple of little rooms, one of which was a study, a big drawing room and a kitchen. So everyone had their own room, but there didn't seem any point to me in getting a place where we could all live in separate rooms. Of course that sometimes created quite a lot of tension. I wouldn't say for a second that it was always easy, I was in tears quite often, but the good times far out-weighed the bad, and I don't regret a day of it.

When we were playing at the Aldwych and staying at Hampstead, we would drive up to Stratford every Saturday night after the performance; no M40 then, so it was quite a long drive. I would cook the Sunday lunch for all of us. We had to buy a toaster every year we were there, which was twelve years. I never knew how they used to break them, but we bought a new one every Easter.

It was the year after that before Michael and I rejoined the RSC, and moved back to Stratford ourselves. After the York disaster, Frank Hauser asked me to return to Oxford for *The Wolf,* written in 1911 by the Hungarian writer Ferenc Molnár. This was another British premiere by Frank for a classic European play unknown here, and it was wonderful to be directed by him again, you just felt totally confident that there was somebody on the bridge. This was his farewell production for the Oxford Play-house after seventeen years, which was one of the reasons I was keen to be in it.

Leo McKern was to play my insanely jealous husband, and Teddy Woodward my lover. We had a scene where we were all drinking, and one night Teddy knocked the bottom of his glass and it broke off, so I handed him mine. Leo said, 'What good's that going to do us?' as we had some stage business with the glasses later on. In the first act Leo had a line, 'I'm so happy,' and a man shouted out, 'Well, I'm glad you are!' But everybody else seemed to enjoy it, with the exception of Finty. She was brought in when I was having a costume fitting, and when she saw me dressed up she burst into tears. She got more used to seeing me like that as she grew up.

The show transferred to London, but we kept getting moved from one theatre to another — the Apollo, the Queen's, and then that barn of a theatre, the New London. We called ourselves the only touring show in London. After six months I called it a day, and left to do my second musical, *The Good Companions,* with a director who was not in the same league as Frank.

Braham Murray seemed all over the shop to me, and I had never done a musical from the beginning before, so I didn't know that it was all rewritten in rehearsal. For *Cabaret*

Hal Prince had ironed out all those usual teething problems during the American run, but now we were starting from scratch. Ronald Harwood had adapted J.B. Priestley's original play, André Previn wrote the music, and the lyrics were by Johnny Mercer. Christopher Gable was in it, and I was so bewitched by working with a real ballet dancer, after my childhood dreams, that all the way through the run I used to try and catch him unawares, and run at him and jump into his arms, so that he could hold me up in that wonderful balletic pose. Poor Chris.

This was the first time that I worked with John Mills, and not many people realised that he was a proper hoofer, he really could tap dance. He had a song and dance number that used to bring the house down. I managed to get to know him really well, because my first entrance was in a little car with John, and we used to sit in it for ages before we were needed, and just talk. It became like a private confessional, and Johnny said, 'Afterwards I'll have this car put in the garden. I've said things to you in this car that I've never said to anyone!'

He and his wife Mary used to invite Michael and me to dinner with them after the show, and because our curtain came down quite late we had to tell the restaurant beforehand what we wanted to eat. So when Johnny came on with a clipboard in one scene, calling, 'Miss Trant, Miss Trant,' he would come up to me with the whole of the menu, and say, 'What do you think you'd like tonight?' We would go right down the menu and choose something, and I would say that Michael would probably have the fishcakes.

Johnny was a man after my own heart. He and I organised a very elaborate practical joke to play on a member of the company who we didn't think was behaving very well. He kept going and looking down at the orchestra, and we were thinking, Oh, come on, there is a show supposed to be going on here. We had a scene at Crewe Station with three big theatre companies all going off in different directions on other trains, with a huge number of suitcases. So we put two stage weights in the case for this particular person, and John had to give them out. Everyone used to take their case and swing it up above their heads, but of course his case was so heavy that it swung away from him and threw him on the floor. John and I laughed so much when we did the scene that afterwards we were helpless with laughter in the corridor, and Ann Way, who was also in that scene, came towards us and said to John, 'I have never seen anything in my life so amateur!' She was quite right of course, but oh gosh, it was an irresistible afternoon. Waiting for it to happen was the best bit, when everyone else picked up theirs, he was dragging his along the floor.

Celia Bannerman was playing Susie, and I thought she was wonderful, but she seemed uneasy about singing the songs. She left suddenly early on, and the understudy had to go on. We worked so hard that night helping the understudy through it, and the next day we got such a dressing-down from Braham Murray. I was so angry that I exploded, 'You must be joking if you think that any of us wouldn't be working hard. You must be *joking,* Braham, if you think that we were all pulling back and not doing our best, with an understudy on, playing the lead!'

It ran for about nine months at Her Majesty's Theatre in the Haymarket, and I think it might have run for longer if it had not been for the spate of IRA bombs in London. I remember one going off in Pall Mall just round the corner. Audiences were understandably not keen to go out while all that was happening.

Then I moved up the road to the Albery, to be directed by my great hero, John Gielgud, in Pinero's *The Gay Lord Quex,* which had been very popular in the early years of the last century. Daniel Massey played the title role, Siân Phillips was his old love the Duchess of Strood, and I played the manicurist Sophy Fullgarney, the role which made the name of Irene Vanbrugh in the first production in 1899. Sir John had seen her act in the Thirties, and had wanted to direct this play for years, but even he came to recognise that it had become very dated. His production had a beautiful look, but it was not a good play.

We rehearsed in the crypt at St James's Church in Piccadilly, and one morning when we had been working for a couple of hours, suddenly out of the loo came a man carrying a pair of trousers, who ran straight through the room and up the stairs. Then came a man not wearing a pair of trousers, who rushed after him straight up the stairs. Sir John laughed so much that he cancelled rehearsals for the rest of the day.

As a director he changed his mind a lot during rehearsals. He would always find a very good reason for giving you a note, and it always seemed to hang together, and then he would come in the next day and it was all out of the window. He would say, 'I don't think anything I gave you yesterday was any good, we'll do something else.' So we had to keep adjusting it, but because we were all completely in awe of him, and wanted so much to work with him, anything he said went, anything was OK by me.

My favourite story of that play happened outside the stage door. Ours was opposite the stage door of Wyndham's Theatre, where John Gielgud was appearing with Ralph Richardson in Harold Pinter's *No Man's Land.* As we were going in one door Sir John happened to be going in the other. He called out, 'Oh, hello, Dan, I hear your play's coming off. No good? Oh my God, I directed it!' Just one more of his famous 'bricks'.

■ ■ ■ ■

7
GOLDEN YEARS AT THE RSC
1975–1981

■ ■ ■ ■

Having bought the house at Charlecote for all the family, it was a relief when Michael and I were able to move back to Stratford and rejoin the RSC for the rest of the Seventies, even if some of the time it meant that we were commuting back and forth to the Aldwych. My first play was in fact scheduled to run there: Shaw's *Too True To Be Good,* which was once again in the skilled hands of Clifford Williams. It is one of Shaw's strangest, with a Microbe in Act I and a send-up of Lawrence of Arabia in Act II. I was originally asked to play the part that was eventually taken by Anna Calder-Marshall, but then I read it and realised that Sweetie Simpkins has a much better time, and I was absolutely right. She has to pretend to be a French Countess, and I had a wonderful time dressing up as the Countess, and putting on a French accent with Sweetie's own Cockney twang breaking through it frequently. Ian McKellen was a burglar turned preacher, and we both had a lot of fun.

There were some challenging Shakespeare plays to come, but we had a very strong company to tackle them — Donald Sinden, Ian McKellen, Michael Pennington, Bob Peck, Robin Ellis, Richard Griffiths, Ian McDiarmid, Griffith Jones, John Woodvine, Greg Hicks, Roger Rees, Nickolas Grace, Mike Gwilym, Barbara Leigh-Hunt, Francesca Annis, Marie Kean, and of course my own Michael, who was going to play *The Good Soldier Schweik* as well as the Shakespeares, and took over the Lawrence part in the Shaw. Somebody later christened that company the 'Golden Ensemble', and it certainly felt like that to all of us at the time.

In *Much Ado About Nothing* Donald was Benedick to my Beatrice. John Barton, who was directing, had the idea of setting it at the time of the British Raj in India, and John had the view that this was the last summer that they would get anything together at all. It was very nice that they weren't young sparring partners, that they weren't quite over the hill, but almost over the hill. Beatrice is a difficult part, because there is this brilliant repartee between them both all the time, and then suddenly she turns and says, 'Kill Claudio.' I used to get a laugh on it, and of course the laugh should not have been there, it should be very shocking and make the audience gasp. I had to work really hard not to get that laugh, I tried the line differently every evening, but still it came more often than it should. Strangely enough, much later on when I directed Kenneth Branagh as Benedick, and Samantha Bond as Beatrice, she never got the laugh at all. (But we will come to my brief foray into directing in a later chapter.)

We all had beautiful and exotic costumes in *Much Ado,* designed by John Napier, and it was a brilliant idea to have John Woodvine play Dogberry as a Sikh in a turban, which made sense of him getting the language wrong. He was hilarious, but he is a terrible practical joker, worse than me, and his jokes made the actors playing the Watch corpse on many nights.

The costumes for *Macbeth* were almost minimal by comparison. It was the play that Ian McKellen and I most wanted to do, but Trevor Nunn was very reluctant. The three of us were having supper in Hampstead, and he said, 'Oh, I've done it so many times I'm not sure I have any new ideas, I think it should be someone else.' Well, he had a mutiny on his hands. I said to Trevor,

'Come on, let's do it, we'll have a laugh.' Eventually he agreed to direct it in The Other Place at Stratford, in a simple production to suit that small space. It was an old shed with a corrugated iron roof, which had been adapted into a small studio theatre. We went to look at it, and walking back to the main theatre I said, 'This is not going to work, is it? It's just not going to work.' And at that moment I fell off the pavement. I got up and walked a bit further and said, 'It really isn't going to work,' and then I fell over again. But that didn't bode ill actually, as it worked like a dream when we got down to it.

The next day we went back for a rehearsal, and Trevor had got the stage management to block out every chink of light with paper stuffed in all the gaps in the corrugated iron roof. He didn't put any lights on and said, 'Ian, go to the top of the stairs. Judi, wait at the bottom. Ian, come down the stairs, knowing there are people asleep all around you, and now play the scene of coming down after the murder.' That seemed to unlock something within us all. The small auditorium could only seat 150 people, and with very little room backstage we were all in one room getting ready. There was a very small cupboard off it, that usually housed wig-boxes, and that was where the girls dressed. We were all cramped in there, while the chaps were in the slightly larger room. But this induced a wonderful company feeling, and an unbelievable air of levity, with lots of stupid schoolboy and schoolgirl jokes. When we actually came to do the play, straight through without an interval, it was a very concentrated piece. That is what creates a company, and an audience will always register if members of a company have a rapport with each other.

The play opened with us all sitting on orange boxes in a circle, and there were no understudies. Roger Rees, who was playing Malcolm, had broken an ankle and was in a wheelchair. The management said, 'Well, you know this is booked out every night.' Roger said, 'If it can be explained, I'll play Malcolm from the wheelchair.' So he came into the circle in the chair, Griffith Jones as Duncan in a white habit and long white beard was helped forward by two people, and then the Witches came on. Susie Dury put on a limp and dragged her leg, and dribbled out of the side of her mouth a bit, followed by the other two. Marie Kean was playing the First Witch, and as she passed she said to me out of the corner of her mouth, 'It's the Lourdes production!' She looked terrifying, and at one point she had to go through the loos to get back onstage, and found some schoolboys hiding in there. She hissed at them, 'What are you doing here? Get out, get out.' She gave them the fright of their lives, and we heard a scuffling in the corner as they came out. I think they regretted skiving off.

The claustrophobic atmosphere in that confined space helped to evoke such a strong sense of evil that we came to recognise a priest in the front row most nights, holding up a crucifix to protect the actors from it. This was Neville Boundy, and it was flattering that he should get so carried away, but it has to be said that he is a very theatrical priest. The production was such a sellout that we had to transfer it to the main house, because of all the complaints that no one could get tickets. But that was a kind of disaster, because it didn't work there at all, it lost its intensity. That was recaptured at the Young Vic when we took it there, because we were back in the right-sized theatre for it.

I never agreed with Edith Evans's belief that there is a scene with Lady Macbeth missing from the play. Just before he speaks to the murderers Macbeth says:

'We will keep ourself
Till supper-time alone: while then, God be
    with you!'

and she leaves him. After he has seen the
murderers, and before the two of them meet
again, her soliloquy says it all:

'Naught's had, all's spent,
Where our desire is got without content:
'Tis safer to be that which we destroy,
Than by destruction, dwell in doubtful joy.'

It charts every bit of the breakdown. Then
you see the beginning of the banquet, when
she is trying to make this tremendous effort, and suddenly the whole thing just
cracks into thousands of pieces. She can't
go on, she answers in single lines from then
on.

That is why it is so important at the beginning that she is not a woman who could do
it on her own. I am always against those
Lady Macbeths who are so strong and evil
at the beginning. If they can do it on their
own, why do they invoke the spirits to help
them? When she says: 'You lack the season
of all natures, sleep,' it tells you absolutely
what has been happening to them. He starts
to exclude her from everything, and obviously paces around alone at night. So it is

right that she disappears from view, and then suddenly you see her with her mind completely gone. I don't see where there could have been another scene, and what it would say that is not already said in the play. I said to Trevor, 'We must play it so that any schoolchildren who come to see it and don't know it will think that they might not do the murder.'

After we finished the run at the Young Vic we recorded it for Thames Television. It was well received on transmission, but I made the great mistake of watching it, and I was desperately disappointed in what I had done. I had imagined that my performance was better than what I saw on the screen. It stopped me watching anything else. I thought, I am not going to watch myself again, I will just have this fantasy in my mind of what I actually do. So there are quite a lot of my films that I have never seen, except for a few premieres I could not avoid.

Many of the *Macbeth* cast were also in *The Comedy of Errors,* which came next, and when John Napier showed us the set for it everybody just burst into applause. It was centred round a Greek taverna, with balconies and tables outside, and at the beginning we all came on and waved to our friends; that was very exciting. When the audience came in, waiters were brushing up in the street and would talk to them. I have never had so many letters from schoolchildren, because they suddenly saw something that was very unstuffy, and they could not believe that it was so immediate and modern, just like a place they might go on holiday. We were very faithful to the play, but it had music and dancing.

Gillian Lynne was the choreographer, and she used to put us through an hour's movement class every morning before we started rehearsing. She even got Trevor Nunn doing it. We all did split leaps across the room, and got very fit, which was necessary as it was a very physical production, running up and down stairs and on to the stage. Gillian was very strict with us, and my Michael got so peeved with her once that he nearly threw a chair at her, but fortunately thought better of it.

That joker John Woodvine took over from Robin Ellis as Dr Pinch, and on the last night he excelled himself. He had an entrance through the audience, and as he came up he turned and said, 'Keep my seat, Aphrodite, I'll be back,' which nearly brought the house down. I had to say, 'Good Doctor Pinch . . .' and before I could finish the line he interrupted, saying, 'I'm not a good doctor, I don't have the patients.' That brought the whole house to a standstill, including all of us.

Somebody used to fire a gun up into the flies, and a bird dropped down, but this night the bird dropped down about six lines later, the whole thing was chaos — the audience loved it. This was the first season when the RSC toured to Newcastle, and at the end when we invited people to come up and join the dance onstage, they stayed dancing for so long that we thought we would never get back to our digs at all. We finally had to say that perhaps it was now time they all went home. The whole experience with that play was a very joyous one.

Which is more than I can say for the next one — *King Lear.* It was my own fault, because originally it was the only play in that season I was not to be in. When I asked Trevor if I could change my mind, he said, 'Yes, I'll put you down to play Regan.' But then I didn't enjoy playing it, and I still don't know why really. I had a wonderful grey fur coat, a grey fur hat and boots, which I thought was frightfully glamorous, until at the dress rehearsal Mike Gwilym and Nick Grace said, 'For goodness' sake don't run in that, or somebody will take a pot-shot at you.'

Donald was wonderful as Lear, and my Michael was quite brilliant as the Fool, but I didn't feel wonderful because it didn't feel right that the three of us playing Lear's daughters were presented as if we were at the State Opening of Parliament at the beginning, in white dresses with blue sashes and tiaras. Somehow I could not reconcile that world with one where someone would come in and say of the bound Gloucester, 'Pluck out his eyes.'

In that scene John Woodvine was not much help as my husband, the Duke of Cornwall. On the first night I just caught a glimpse out of the corner of my eye as he took something out of a plastic bag with his back to the audience. Then as he said, 'Out, vile jelly,' he threw this eye, which flew across the stage and stuck on the side of the proscenium arch. At that moment I thought it was faintingly frightful, what a wonderful effect. But the next night I came on, and saw the eye from the night before, still stuck on the proscenium arch, and thought this was not promising for the rest of the run. When the production transferred to the Aldwych I asked to be released from that part. I found it just as unpleasant as playing Portia.

My memories of the next two plays I did at the Aldwych are hazy in the extreme. In Ibsen's *Pillars of the Community* I played Lona Hessel to Ian McKellen's Karsten Bernick, and I only had three short scenes. All I can remember is that I had red boots, whistled, and had a vaguely tartan dress; I can't recall a single thing about the story. As for Congreve's *The Way of the World,* I never understood the plot, either in rehearsal or in performance — and fortunately there were not too many of those. The best thing about it was playing Millamant opposite Michael Pennington as Mirabell. We were to co-star several times in the coming years. The next time was in *The Gift of the Gorgon* by Peter Shaffer, when we played Mr and Mrs Damson, so after those two plays we always greet each other now as Mr and Mrs Plum.

I felt that I was in for a run of difficult parts when I went back to Stratford to play Imogen in *Cymbeline.* I had seen Dame Peggy play it at Stratford in the Fifties, and I thought she was exquisite. So I went to ask her advice, which was not the most comforting: 'It's an absolute pig of a part, I never got it right. You'll hate playing it each night, but on the last night you'll regret not being able to play it again.' I agreed with her about the part, but not about the re-grets.

Cymbeline is difficult to make sense of, being a kind of fairy tale, with an evil queen and a heroine, and a great cross-section of characters. My worst memory of it is of the scene where Imogen wakes up beside what she thinks is the body of her husband with his head cut off. Bernard Shaw wrote a whole essay on how unfair it was to put the actress in that position, and I was inclined to agree. I was not helped by the fact that the dummy in my arms had knees that bent in both directions, so it was very tricky to manoeuvre without getting unwanted laughs. David Jones was the director, but he had to leave for America as soon as we opened, so he wasn't around to help us get it right. In the end I think we got away with it, but it is not a play for which I have any affection.

So I was much relieved to get to work on Sean O'Casey's *Juno and the Paycock,* which we did at the Aldwych. I loved the challenge of doing an Irish play with an all-Irish cast, and I thought, Now I will see where my roots are, with a mother from Dublin, and a father who spent much of his early life there. It was a great help to have old friends like Marie Kean and Norman

141

Rodway in the cast, and I quickly made new friends of the others, especially Dearbhla Molloy, who was playing my daughter.

Trevor gave it a very realistic production, and I had to cook a sausage onstage for Norman. There was not actually enough time to cook it properly, so I had to palm it and substitute a cooked one, but I had so many people asking, 'Is Norman all right, eating that half-cooked sausage?' The last scene is a highly emotional peak, where Juno has a huge long speech to her husband saying, 'Why, why have I been accused?' I was reluctant to commit myself to it for quite a while. There has always been a kind of funny superstition about doing the last scene of a play, and in the past there were actors who would never say the last line of any play in rehearsal.

But Trevor took me through it just like he did in *The Winter's Tale*. One afternoon he said, 'Come on, we'll go into the theatre,' and the two of us did it. It is a wonderful way of working, just doing it really step by step, and doing it privately, so that nobody else had to be around. If you can analyse it and quietly do it with the director, then it doesn't become a fearful thing. I became mad about the play, and we had a great run in it. One notice said that I was unrecognisable in the part, which was music to my ears, I could not have wished for anything else.

During those early rehearsals of *Juno,* when I couldn't get it right, I said to Trevor, 'Oh, why can't I play some mangy old cat in this thing you're doing?' This was the Andrew Lloyd Webber musical *Cats,* based on T.S. Eliot's *Old Possum's Book of Practical Cats,* which Trevor was directing next. So they asked me to play Grizabella and the Gumbie Cat. Gillian Lynne was doing the choreography, and we rehearsed in a funny old gym in Chiswick. Brian Blessed was also in it, and we had to do classes with all the dancers, but quite often Gillie would say to us, 'Brian and Judi, don't do this.' Then one morning, rehearsing the Gumbie Cat with Wayne Sleep, I just heard this huge crack. I knew what it was, because it had happened to Nick Grace during *The Comedy of Errors.* It is unbelievably painful when it happens, just like an enormous, huge piece of furniture being smashed against the back of your leg. I turned to see who had kicked me. You hear what sounds like a pistol-shot going off, and it is just like a carthorse kicking you in the back of the leg. I knew straight away, and so did everybody else. Wayne Sleep just picked me up and carried me, I don't know how he did it. I was taken home, and had a bath with difficulty. Then I was driven off to the surgeon Justin Howse, who said, 'I'm afraid you've snapped your Achilles tendon, you must come in tomorrow and have it operated on.' I asked him, 'How long is that?' and he said, 'Six weeks.' I thought, Ohhhh!

Michael was away in France, playing the assistant to Derek Jacobi's KGB chief in the spy film *Enigma,* so I said to Bonnie, our nanny, 'If Mike phones, don't tell him till it's done.' I was in hospital for two weeks at the Fitzroy Nuffield Clinic in Bryanston Square. Trevor and Andrew came to see me and said, 'We'll delay the opening, you obviously can't now play the Gumbie Cat, but you can play Grizabella, because she's meant to be clapped-out, it doesn't matter.' So I went back to rehearsals, which had now moved into the New London Theatre. I went to see Trevor the day before, to brush up on the song. The next day we were going to do the beginning, and I walked up those platforms on to the stage and fell off. I couldn't manoeuvre them. So I went to my dressing room, called a taxi, and went home to Hampstead. Michael was home, but he was going back that day to Strasbourg. I rang Trevor and said, 'Trevor, we have to be practical, there is no way I can do this.' So they recast it, and Elaine Paige took over as Grizabella.

Michael's film director, Jeannot Szwarc, said to him, 'I think we ought to get Judi out of England for the opening of *Cats*, I don't think she should be around for all that razzamatazz,' as the word was that it was going to be very special. So he invited Finty and me to Paris, and we went, but by then I had to dress my leg each day. We came back from Paris, and I will always remember this: at the airport that morning as we were leaving, all the moving walkways had stopped, and we had to walk. There was a very nice man who took my case for me, I don't know who he was. Then I went to see Justin Howse and he said, 'Oh Christ, this is no good.'

We were going to dinner with Mary and John Mills at his club, and Justin said, 'No, no, something terrible's happening, you'll have to come back in again, I'll have to re-operate on it.' So the four of us had a rather tearful dinner. The next day I went into the Nightingale Clinic in Lisson Grove, and I was going to have the operation the day after, but when he looked at it then it had completely burst and drained. He said, 'In actual fact, I'm not going to have to do that at all, something quite extraordinary has happened to it. What you will have to do, though, is just to lie there.'

I lay there for a month and a day, and watched television. I never was interested in Wimbledon before, and I have always loved it ever since, because it really was a lifesaver. I used to read, and I had lots of visitors coming to see me. It was then that I realised how tiring it is to lie in bed. John Stride and April and their little daughter Nell came to see me, and Nell took all her clothes off in a wonderful kind of cabaret.

One of the nicest calls I received in hospital was from Hal Prince, who heard about what had happened and rang me from America to say, 'I'll tell you exactly what you're going to do after you come out of there. You and Finty and Mike are going to come to our house in Majorca. We're going to be there for the summer — come and have a holiday.' So that is what we did; we had never had a summer holiday before that, and that was where we met Stephen Sondheim for the first time. He was swimming in the pool, and Hal just said, 'This is Steve,' and we didn't know who he was until he was playing the piano later, and Michael said to me, 'Hello, you know who Steve is, don't you?' We had a lovely holiday there, it was very kind of Hal and Judy, and ever after that we made sure we had a summer holiday, because we realised that it is absolutely essential to get the batteries going again.

When we got back from Majorca, *Cats* had become a smash-hit, and we finally went to see it on 9 September 1981 — I can always remember that date. Although I suppose I cried a little bit, I saw how wonderful Elaine Paige was in it, and I had no regrets about it. I thought I would find it really painful, but I didn't at all.

■ ■ ■ ■ ■

8
FROM LADY
BRACKNELL TO
MOTHER COURAGE
1982–1985

■ ■ ■ ■

In 1982 I went to the National Theatre for the first time, at Peter Hall's invitation. There had always been a kind of rivalry between the Royal Shakespeare Company and the National Theatre, you were seen as either an RSC actor or a National Theatre actor. Now, I can't imagine why, but there was then this division between us all. I was glad to be asked by Peter, as I wanted to go to the National very much, and I didn't feel that I was somehow betraying the RSC. After all, Peter had moved from one to the other, and he was the bridge between them.

He was going to direct *The Importance of Being Earnest,* and wanted me to play Lady Bracknell. Several people warned me off the part, and Peggy Ashcroft came round to my house in Hampstead with George Rylands and said, 'This is a part you mustn't play, you mustn't play this part. You really mustn't.' She never told me why, and I was too frightened to ask, because I was committed to play it by then. So I didn't want to find out why. I knew that Peggy had played Cecily to Edith Evans's famous dragon of a Lady Bracknell in 1939, and I think she thought, like many people, that invidious comparisons would be drawn.

Zoë Wanamaker was playing Gwendolen in this production, and we already knew that we were both going to be together again in *Mother Courage* for the RSC, so I used to stand in the wings with her and say, 'We must make the best of this, because we could be pulling that cart round the stage. We must get on and make the best of it.'

But I found it quite difficult at the beginning to find the character of Lady Bracknell. I said to Peter, 'I feel too young to play this,' and he said, 'You can say that once more, and then you're not to say that again.' That was very good for me. Then I had a couple of weeks off while they set Act II, which I wasn't in, and Michael and I drove up to Scotland for a holiday. We stopped at Inveraray for lunch, and I looked at the Castle, which gave me an inspiration. I suddenly thought, I know exactly how to play her: like Margaret, Duchess of Argyll, with that very pale face, dark hair, and red mouth. I had never met her, but had read all those stories in the newspapers about her love affairs. I thought that there was a similar quality in Lady Bracknell of being quite predatory. She is so awful about Lord Bracknell, and I thought that she was always dying to get round to Half Moon Street, to have her hand on Algy's knee. Nigel Havers was playing Algy, and Martin Jarvis was Jack Worthing.

I gave Martin a terrible fright on Boxing Night. The shower in my dressing room suddenly went on the blink, boiling water absolutely poured out, and I couldn't stop it. I couldn't get anyone to fix it, and then I was called to go onstage. Martin was leading up to his line, 'I was found, Lady Bracknell,' when I skipped half a page and cut his first reference to the handbag. It gave him quite a turn — I saw the whites of his eyes. Of course it had to be the most famous line I cut: 'A Handbag!?' Everybody remembered Edith Evans's swooping delivery of it, so it was the great hurdle for me, that was why the dam burst at the weakest point.

We worried for the rest of the evening that the cut would make nonsense of the unravelling of the plot at the end, but it seemed as if few people in the audience noticed. However, one lady did, and wrote to me to say, 'You have ruined my entire Christmas.'

Well, it ruined mine too, so I wrote back to tell her what happened in my dressing room that made me skip that vital bit of the plot. Apart from that particular night, we had a great success with *The Importance.*

Once it had opened, we started rehearsing for the Harold Pinter triple-bill *Other Places* with the same group of actors. I was only in *A Kind of Alaska,* as the girl with sleeping sickness who doesn't wake up for sixteen years. I read up about the disease and its treatment with the drug L-Dopa; when we did it, sixteen sleeping-sickness patients still remained at Enfield Highlands hospital. I also knew that Ralph Richardson's first wife had died of it. All I remember of the first night was that moment of getting out of bed and walking towards Paul Rogers as the doctor, and having an absolutely clear flash of thinking that was why I snapped my Achilles tendon in *Cats,* so that I would know the whole process of learning to walk again. You have to be told to put your heel down, because you are so frightened when you start to walk again. That experience stood me in incredibly good stead. The production was later televised, but the TV director flatly refused to use any of the original cast, and I was very upset about that.

Only being in the last of the three plays meant that Anna Massey and I had time to build an elaborate joke on Nigel and Martin. We let it be known to them that Peter was directing us in another play, entitled *The Crew,* written by a man called Nicholas Harrad, and they got frightfully beady about it. They kept asking us what it was about, and we told them it was about two female lorry drivers. Peter Hall and the stage manager Diana Boddington went along with the act, putting notices and rehearsal schedules up on the notice boards, so Martin and Nigel got more and more jumpy the longer it went on, muttering, 'Why are they being employed and we're not?' I had a photograph taken with me leaning out of a lorry wearing a cap, with a fag hanging out of my mouth, talking to David Hare in a sweater emblazoned *Anna Massey and Judi Dench 'The Crew' by Nicholas Harrad.* I don't know how long it fooled Martin and Nigel, but it was wonderful fun while it lasted.

I also don't know whether that kind of hoax is catching, but the boys were as bad as the girls at setting them up. When we went on tour with *The Importance,* Martin played a dreadful trick on Nigel in Glasgow. Between the matinee and the evening performance Martin changed all the clocks, and he had taped the sound of the audience arriving at the beginning of the show. Nigel was sitting in his dressing room with curlers in his hair, thinking he had got plenty of time to get ready, and Martin played the tape of the curtain going up. Nigel knew he had to get down the stairs, under the stage and up the other side, and he was screaming and throwing the curlers off. Any other man would have had a heart attack. He ran on to the stage, and we were all standing there waiting for him, with the safety curtain down. He was completely shattered. Nigel told me later that it was because he used to pull a trick on Martin, who had said, 'I'll get back at you for this.'

After Wilde and Pinter, my next playwright was Hugh Whitemore, in *Pack of Lies,* which was based on the real-life story of the Portland spy ring run by the Krogers and Gordon Lonsdale, and its effects on their unsuspecting neighbours, played by Michael and me. Apparently the script had been turned down by several other actresses before it was sent to me. Michael read it and said, 'Just read these two lines in Act II.' So I read the two lines and said, 'Oh yes, I would do that.' Since I am notorious for not reading scripts I always relied on his judgement, and he was never wrong. This time he was very enthusiastic, and went off to Ruislip to find the house where Mr and Mrs Search, the real-life couple we were playing, had lived. He had terrible difficulty finding the house, and the rooms were tiny.

Ralph Koltai had designed the set to exactly the same proportions, and we could never think how you could get more than three or four seats in that little front room. When Michael came back he told me there were thirteen chairs in that room. Bill Search still lived there on his own, and he told Michael how his wife had died in the kitchen sitting in a chair, and that scene was put in the play. The Searches were renamed the Jacksons in the script, and my character, the wife Barbara, was a very shy person. Projecting that quality to the circle and upper circle of the Lyric Theatre was really difficult, a very good kind of lesson to do every night. It was a fantastically exciting play, but I did find my part draining. I used to say that I longed to come down the stairs and say, 'My Lord of Warwick . . .' or something like that, because Barbara's horizons were quite contained.

My great friend since the Old Vic days, Barbara Leigh-Hunt, was playing the spy Helen who betrays their friendship. Richard Vernon played the MI5 man who comes to tell the Jacksons who their friends really are, and to ask their help in catching them out. He had to come in at one point and say, 'We're looking for a car, a Vauxhall, with the registration number ABY 129; have you any knowledge of that?' One day he came in and said, 'We're looking for a car, a Vauxhall with the registration number RU 12.' (That is less funny on the page than it sounded on the stage: 'Are you one too?') Well, I had to go off and stand in the hall for a few moments to recover myself.

It was an enormous help that Michael was playing my husband, although we never talked about the theatre or work when we came home; perhaps a little bit in the car, but very little even then. I don't like to talk about a part outside rehearsal whilst I am still working on it. It takes the edge off the spontaneity for me.

While we were both playing in *Pack of Lies,* our first TV sitcom *A Fine Romance* was being transmitted by London Weekend Television. At Christmas we had a row about the sink blocking up at our house in Hampstead. We were being driven to the theatre in a cab, and we were not speaking at all. Going down Shaftesbury Avenue before we turned into the Lyric the cab stopped at some lights, and when a lady passing suddenly caught sight of us she came right up to the window and started to sing 'A fine romance, with no kisses', which ended our row of course.

When Michael and I were first approached to do that television series, Trevor Nunn said, 'Oh no, don't do a situation comedy, that doesn't get bums on seats.' Well, I think he wouldn't say that now. I think it is our business to do as many things as we can, and my goodness it teaches you something. People should not demean situation comedy, it is the most difficult thing in the world.

We played Mike and Laura, a middle-aged couple who are both very shy and fall in love. Bob Larbey had written the scripts, and I was so nervous about it that I asked if the director could be James Cellan-Jones, as I knew how good he was at directing comedy. Michael read it and said, 'You know, this would be hugely good fun.' The other couple were Susan Penhaligon as my young married sister, and Richard Warwick as her husband. We all got on so well that we used to arrange day-trips to France for the cast and crew just as an outing, and everyone else thought we were filming. 'Oh no, we're just here for pleasure.'

What I quickly learnt was why situation

comedy is much more difficult than anything else. You have just five days to rehearse
it before the recording, and then you have
to come out and talk to this big studio audience before you start. I never got used to
that; Michael took to it absolutely without a
hitch, but I was all over the shop. Every
performance that we did, I stood there saying, 'How have I got myself into this?' I love
people coming, but it is just so unlike me to
have to go and say a few lines as myself and
meet the audience, I loathe it. It is like my
worst nightmare, like walking into a room-
ful of people at a party that I don't know. I
dread it, and people just think you are af-
fected if you say that. Making a speech, oh
crikey! But why should it be anything like
acting? Acting is the antithesis of making a
speech, because what you are doing is being
another person, saying lines that somebody
else has told you to.

You have to come out and say, 'Hello, so
nice to see you here, do clap, do enjoy your
evening,' and then you have to suddenly
think about what you are doing in this
scene. There is always the risk of things going wrong, and Michael was a very steady-
ing influence. You have to stop, and say to
the audience, 'Sorry, we're going to have to
go back on this,' and you go back on it and

get it right, and the audience go absolutely mad because you have got it right at last, and then you have to say, 'Don't do that, because we can't have that kind of reaction suddenly in the middle of a scene for no reason.'

In the second episode of *A Fine Romance* I had to pick up some glasses of beer and take them over to a table. In rehearsal I took two in each hand, but when it came to the take I tried to lift all four in one hand. Why would I do that? Fright, it is fright that makes you do it.

We rehearsed in a church hall near Waterloo Bridge. I was walking to the loo and back, singing, and I met the vicar, who said, 'Don't sing in church.' I thought that was a rather rum thing for a vicar to say. We were there on our wedding anniversary, 5 February, and Michael, unbeknownst to me, went over to the man who used to sell flowers underneath the bridge, Buster Edwards, who was one of the Great Train Robbers, and said, 'Could I have a dozen roses, please?' Buster said, 'A dozen roses, mate!! Do you know what time of year this is? Pull yourself together.' Michael was really told off.

The programme was very popular, and for years afterwards people would ask, 'Why don't you do it again?' After four series we decided to call it a day, and the Head of London Weekend Television, John Birt, tried to change our minds. He took us out and asked us why didn't we want to do more. We said we wouldn't do more on television, but why didn't we make a film of it? But nobody seemed at all interested in pursuing that idea.

A Fine Romance appealed to an audience that had never seen us in the theatre, and those who then came to see us in *Pack of Lies* hoped that they were going to see those two dotty people. We had a group of American college students who came to one of the TV recordings, and one of them asked, 'Miss Dench, do you ever get a chance to do any classical theatre?' What could I say but, 'Oh yes, once or twice.'

One famous modern classical role I regretted accepting was Mother Courage for the RSC at the Barbican. Howard Davies had come to tell me the story, but as I had not read the script what I didn't know — and Howard had omitted to tell me — was that she is never off the stage. I was so cross when I found this out on the first day of rehearsal that I said, 'Well, who translated this? I can't make head nor tail of it.' Howard said, 'Hanif Kureishi, this is him here.' Hanif has never spoken to me since.

I thought that I should really not have said yes to this, that this was a big mistake. But then of course we started to work on it, when the anger or fright is turned into adrenalin, and gradually ideas form. People often ask, 'Don't you have difficulty learning the lines?' Sometimes I do have a lot of difficulty learning the lines, but the real difficulty is working out why the character says the line, and what is going on between the lines, which is often more important than the line itself.

Before you start to rehearse you are looking at the wood, which is composed of many trees. You start rehearsing and you are inside the wood; you know that you are in a wood, but you don't know what the trees round you are until you start to recognise them. Then the moment the audience comes in, it is as if you have been transported away from the wood, and that is when I think the most important part comes in — when you decide which is the straightest way through the wood. This is part of the economy of presenting a character, because I think what you leave out is more important than what you put in.

I had admired John Napier's work ever since we had worked together at Stratford, and his set design for *Mother Courage* looked absolutely beautiful, but the engineering of the machinery was faulty, so my cart that trundled around on rails never worked properly. One night it did just one circle of the stage and suddenly one wheel stuck, so it wouldn't move at all. I went forward and made a speech to the audience, 'Look, we are the RSC, not the RAC, so I'm afraid we can't fix this wheel, and you'll have to come back another night.' I thought it was quite funny, but the audience were furious, and they didn't laugh. Zoë Wanamaker was playing my daughter Kattrin, and she and I raced in the car from the Barbican to Joe Allen's restaurant in Covent Garden for an early supper. I was meeting Michael later for another supper, but it didn't matter. Zoë said, 'So this is what Joe Allen's looks like on a Tuesday evening at ten past eight.'

But the cart did break down so many times, and at the end as I was going off to war and was supposed to be pushing it on my own, I had to have four or five stage-hands helping me push it; a great help for me at the time, but not much help to the story. The whole thing was very hard work. I loved all the singing, but I didn't like plucking the chicken — that was horrible, and I didn't know how to do it.

I found in a skip the overcoat that Michael had worn as the Fool in *King Lear,* which I wore at rehearsal, and it worked so well I kept it for the performance. I had clearly in my mind that the wig should be red, and look as if just anybody had cut it, so that it was always standing on end. I was convinced about that, and said so to Lindy Hemming, our costume designer, on the first day, and she produced one exactly like that. Then I couldn't bear to part with it.

We did a run-through as rehearsals were almost over when I thought I had got near to the right performance, but Howard bawled me out afterwards, saying, 'The thing about her is you mustn't make her a heroine.' I don't understand about the Brechtian alienation; I know what he means, I've read about it and understood it, what I don't understand is how you involve the audience with the character's personal predicament. They all spoke about Helene Weigel in the Berliner Ensemble production, and that moment where she heard of the death of her son; well, if what she did is alienation, then I don't understand what the word is.

The boys used to have to give me money for the drinks I sold from the cart, and at one matinee they gave me American Express cards instead of money. So in the evening I had vinegar put in the drinks which they had to knock back, and they all spat it out in a great spray.

After the physical strain of *Mother Courage* it was lovely that the other play in the repertoire was *Waste* by Harley Granville-Barker, about a sexual scandal in the Edwardian era. I had two very nice, neat little scenes, both in the first half, so a lot of nights I used to go home at the interval, because traditionally if you don't appear in the second half you are allowed to do that. But now I don't think I should have done really.

Stephen Moore was with me in *Mother Courage* but not in *Waste,* so we were surprised one night early in the run when he strolled across the set in a dinner jacket. The audience saw nothing strange in that. But I noticed, and when he was playing Captain Hook in *Peter Pan* at the Barbican I thought I would pay him a return visit, dressed as a pirate. I wore my wonderful red lavatory brush of a wig as Mother Courage, borrowed a pair of trousers and a leather jacket, added a patch over one eye and a great big red beard, and joined the other pirates onstage. I stood right in front of Stephen and he didn't even notice me. Then I didn't know how to get off. Stephen can play anything from Brecht to Ayckbourn, with a special gift for comedy, but neither of us has yet had the chance to repeat those unscheduled walk-ons.

Waste was such a success that it transferred to the West End, and I was back at the Lyric again. It was during the run there that I was offered the part of Cleopatra, and was faced with the difficult decision of choosing between two directors, both of whom I admired and had worked with before.

9
CARRIE POOTER AND
CLEOPATRA
1986–1987

It was at the last-night party for *The Importance of Being Earnest* at the National Theatre that Peter Hall said to me, 'You ought to play Cleopatra, but we've got to find the right Antony.' I said, 'Yes, how wonderful, how lovely that would be, and it's so far away it doesn't get alarming yet.' Not long after that Terry Hands also said to me, 'You ought to play Cleopatra,' and I said, 'How absolutely wonderful, yes, how lovely.'

I didn't think much more about it, until in the middle of *Waste* suddenly there were two productions of *Antony and Cleopatra* announced, and I was asked to play her in both of them. I was in the most terrible state about it, and I asked Terry to drop by and see me. When he did, I told him, 'Terry, I did promise Peter first,' and he said, 'Yes, but that was at a party, it wasn't in an office, it wasn't a proper offer.'

I felt extremely badly about that, it was only because I was so flattered to be asked to play it that I was foolish enough to say yes to two people. Terry and Peter had rather a row over it, which made me so upset that I said I wouldn't play it at all. Then Terry wrote me a long letter saying that I must do it, even if it wasn't for him.

Before the National production could go into rehearsal I was committed to something very different — *Mr and Mrs Nobody,* playing Carrie Pooter opposite Michael, with Ned Sherrin directing. I was longing to do it, because I knew and loved the original book, *The Diary of a Nobody* by George and Weedon Grossmith, and Michael and I mistakenly thought it would be an absolute breeze. We played all the speaking parts, Penny Ryder played the maid, and Gary Fairhall was the general factotum; they mimed everything, and did most of the hard work. But it was fantastically hard for all of us; at one point I was wearing three costumes on top of each other because the changes were so quick, we often only had seconds to do them. I lost a lot of weight during the run, which was a great help for Cleopatra.

It was a glorious piece of writing by Keith Waterhouse, and I loved working with Ned.

To begin with, I couldn't believe he would want to work with me, because he had worked so often in association with Caryl Brahms as his co-writer, and she simply loathed me. She wrote a series of notices which would have seared your eyebrows off. One said of me: 'as Juliet she conveys about as much as an apple in a Warwickshire orchard'; and another about Isabella: 'this performance is better than I dared hope, but Rosalind Iden should have played the part'. She used to make dismissive references to 'Dench J.', as if I were still at school, though I am glad to say that in the end we became quite good friends just before she died, after she saw *Macbeth.*

Ned's rehearsals were such good fun, he was precise, and funny, and very astute; then suddenly he would sit back and say, 'The Williamses are on automatic pilot.'

During the run Kenneth Branagh rang up and said, 'I want to see you, will you meet me?' I thought he was going to ask me to do something, and I would have to say no because I was committed to play Cleopatra. But instead he astonished me by saying, 'Would you direct *Much Ado*?' I talked about it to Peter Hall, who said, 'Absolutely, go on, you've got to do it.' So I did, and I learnt a lot from that experience, which I will explain in the next chapter.

The reviews for *Mr and Mrs Nobody* were mixed, but the audiences loved it, and we ran for over four months before I had to go back to the National to start rehearsals for *Antony and Cleopatra.* By then Peter had got his Antony — Anthony Hopkins, who had just played two punishing leading roles at the National in David Hare's *Pravda,* and *King Lear.* Tony had never read the play before, and nor had I, though I had seen Peggy Ashcroft play it with Michael Redgrave at Stratford years ago.

I was always anxious about playing her, because whenever I said I was going to play Cleopatra people used to openly laugh in my face. 'Cleopatra? You?' So I was really paranoid about it, and at the first rehearsal I said to Peter, 'Well, I hope you know what you are doing, setting out to direct *Cleopatra* with a menopausal dwarf.'

But Peter was in marvellous form for it. I remember a reading we had up in the conference room, and he was so enthusiastic. After the reading he said, 'Oh, it's going to be rather marvellous,' and that was a great boost to our morale. He stood at a lectern with his script, and it was like being conducted in an opera, it was very exciting. He made the story really clear. I found out lots of things about her, that she was pregnant, for instance, when the news came that Antony had been married in Rome. Peter gave me two notes which I still pass on to all students. The first was: 'Don't think that you've got to come in and play all of Cleopatra in the first scene. All you do is play aspects of her in all the scenes, and by the end hopefully you'll have the whole character.' That is a wonderful note to be given, and actually it applies to any part in any play.

The second note was when I was worrying about how I could possibly live up to Enobarbus's great speech about her: 'the barge she sat in . . .' Peter said, 'Don't believe everything that everybody says about you in the play. Enobarbus is only back in Rome with his mates in the pub, having a drink, and they are all asking, "What's she like, what's she like?" So of course he's going to say, "My God, you could smell the perfume coming across." ' That put a whole different complexion on it. The truth of it is that everyone is saying all this about them, and suddenly you see these two people who are behaving like real shits, behaving really badly.

It was important to keep the momentum and the truth of the story alive, and one way to do that was not to set anything too much. Because Tony and I changed our moves every time in rehearsal, Peter asked, 'Do you want to settle this? Do you want me to set it, or shall we just leave it fluid?' Neither of us spoke at all for a minute, because neither of us knew what the other one wanted to say, and then both of us said, 'Can we just leave it fluid?' That meant we had to have follow-spots on us, because sometimes Tony would walk out one way, and sometimes he would not walk on at all, so we didn't quite know where the other person was going to jump. It kept the whole thing fresh.

Peter told the girls, 'Just go with Cleopatra, go where she goes, and stop when she stops, it should be like a shoal of fish.' When we were going to rehearse the first scene, Tony and I arrived early that morning, before all the others, and we rolled about on the floor a lot. Just before the first run-through I found a penny and put it in my bag. I touched that penny before we did every run-through, and then I had it sewn into my dress. I am not really superstitious, but I know the reasons for many of those old theatre traditions, like not having real flowers onstage because actors slipped on them.

Peter was a stickler for the verse, as one should be. He said, 'If you actually adhere to verse-speaking in this way, it will never let you down, you will never run out of breath. You will never suffer that problem where your voice becomes so thin and strained because you just haven't got enough breath to push it to the end of the line. If you obey the caesura in the middle of the line, and somebody ends on a half-line, then you must answer exactly, so that it makes up the full line.'

When Helen Fitzgerald, Miranda Foster and I were rehearsing the death of Cleopatra with her maids, Peter was there at the lectern hammering out the beat to get it right. We were the whole morning doing it, and at the end we finally came to the bit about 'our royal lady's dead', and there was a pause, and Peter said, 'Thank Christ!'

He warned me that the great challenge is that she has got to have a fifth gear, which has not been seen yet, and it is what she goes into after Antony dies, a kind of overdrive, and it wasn't until I did it that I understood what he meant. She becomes another person really. After we had been running for about three months, Peter came back and said the production had got a bit baroque, and I knew exactly what that meant, when you embellish things.

I needed to get used to the snakes, too. I am not really frightened of snakes, only worms, but it was difficult. Michael told me just to give them names, then I wouldn't be so frightened. Peter said that the visual impact of this dead woman with the snakes still alive in her hand was very potent on stage. So we auditioned some snakes. The blindworms didn't get the part — much too wormy — but the garter snakes did. We had two of them, and one of them escaped during the run and got into the back of the set of *A Small Family Business* which Michael Gambon was doing at the time. The snake I used on the first night sloughed its skin the night before, and I thought, Don't we all sleep with fright? But it looked absolutely beautiful, it looked like the paint department had got to it.

The fear factor was pretty high for all of us. I remember saying to Tony on the first night, 'People are being born and dying at this minute; we're just doing a play, that's all we're doing.' That first night was one of the happiest first nights I have ever had, because there was so much to remember, and I like that. I like being given notes just before the first night, I love it. First of all there was the prejudice about me playing the part in the first place, and there were so many things to think about, not least being thrown off the monument. It was a vast undertaking, but the first night of *Antony and Cleopatra* was the best performance we had given of it so far, and we didn't think, as we sometimes do, Oh, the dress rehearsal was better.

Getting up into the monument was not so difficult — it was getting down which was tricky. On the first day Peter said, 'I don't know how we are going to do this. There are some stairs, I suppose you could come down there.' I said, 'Get rid of the stairs, you'll think up a way of coming down.' It shouldn't be a careful moment, it should be a desperate one. So I was passed down a lot of strong hands.

Miranda, Helen and I were up in the monument for twenty minutes, during the scene where Antony's servant Eros runs on his own sword, and as we sat in the dark we would talk about what ideally we would like to eat. For me it was always seafood and a glass of champagne, I was very boring about it. On the very last night, as we climbed up into the monument, the other two went up quite quickly, and when I stepped inside this dark gloom they had tiny little torches which they switched on, and there were three dressed crabs and half a bottle of champagne, and we sat there and ate it. We had to wait for Tony's shout below us so that we could pull the cork on the champagne.

He never minded not being in the fifth act; far from it, he loved it. In his death scene at the top of the monument, as he was lying there cradled in my arms, he used to whisper,

'I'm going upstairs to have a nice cup of tea. You do Act V, and I'll have a nice cup of tea.'

We never knew how big the armies were going to be each night. There would be an announcement on the tannoy back-stage asking for volunteers to be part of the Egyptian and the Roman army, from anyone playing in the Lyttelton or the Cottesloe who wasn't on. So, depending on which other plays were in the repertoire that night, sometimes we would get a huge army, and sometimes we would only get about six people, and they would rush across the big Olivier stage from downstage left to upstage right, and there was very little time, because they had to change their colours for the different armies.

My dresser Lou was an aroma therapist, so between a matinee and the evening performance she used to give me a marvellous aromatherapy massage, and I never used to wash the stuff off, because I thought it was so right that Cleopatra should have this musk-like smell.

We had wonderful costumes designed by Alison Chitty, who put the Romans in steel-greys and blues and white, very pale, cold colours, and all of Egypt was in orange, yellow and pink, earth colours. There were beautifully made tassels for the Egyptians, and when Antony went back to Rome in his armour Alison gave him one of her tassels to hang from his belt, which told the whole story of the loucheness of Egypt, and him going back into this very upright, buttoned-up society in Rome.

That production was memorable in so many ways. When I was opening my mail one morning I spotted a very official-looking envelope, and I thought it was a summons, so I stuffed it unopened in my bag with all the other summonses and parking tickets. When I opened it during the matinee I had a really severe shock. I had to read it several times before it sunk in that I was going to be made a Dame of the British Empire in the New Year's Honours. Of course I couldn't tell anybody, though I did tell Michael and swore him to secrecy. Tony

Hopkins's birthday is on 31 December, so that night all the dressing-room windows were thrown open for rousing choruses of first 'Happy Birthday' and then 'There is Nothing like a Dame'.

Earlier that month several of us took part in a gala at the Old Vic to celebrate the eightieth birthday of Dame Peggy Ashcroft. Tim Pigott-Smith, who was playing Octavius in our play, had appeared with Peggy in *Jewel in the Crown,* and he did a very funny version of 'The one-eyed yellow idol to the north of Kathmandu', dressed as his character in that TV series, wearing one black glove to indicate Merrick's prosthetic hand. I pulled his leg about that, and rashly said to Tim, 'That's strangely attractive, that black leather glove.' The next night he wore one glove as Octavius in the last scene, and I pretended not to notice. So next he hid it in the basket with the asp, which did make me gasp. Well, that was literally throwing down the gauntlet.

It became a challenge to return it in the most unexpected places — I had it handed to him onstage in *Mary Stuart,* it fell out of my parasol when I opened it in *A Little Night Music,* Tim had it stencilled on the window in my dressing-room loo, I had it made up in the form of a chocolate cake for his birthday, and when I couldn't go to his wedding anniversary lunch at the Ivy I sent him a white tureen with a lid and a beautiful china ladle, with the glove lying in the bottom. Much later on, he came to see *Hay Fever,* and arranged with Dan Stevens to give it to me onstage, but I knew he was in, so I came in from the garden wearing one. Tim thought he had caught me out, and sent a message to Dan saying, 'Well done!' and Dan had to confess, 'But I haven't had a chance to give it to her yet!'

When Peter Hall asked us both to be in the Gala Opening of the new Rose Theatre at Kingston in 2004, I got the stage manager to summon Tim on the tannoy back to the stage just after he had rehearsed his scene. I hid in the circle, and when he came on, puzzled as to why he'd been called back so quickly, I threw the glove at his feet. Then it dawned on him, and he looked up and grinned at me, 'Thus it goes on.' And so it has, to this day. This silly game has become so well known that whenever I am questioned by an audience someone always asks, 'Where is the glove now?' Everyone seems to get as much fun out of it as we do, so it seems a shame to stop. At that Gala performance in Kingston Tim brought the house down with a wickedly funny impression of

Alan Bennett in his sketch *Going Round.*

The last night of *Antony and Cleopatra* was absolutely wonderful. Peggy Ashcroft came on at the end, and we were all given roses. We had all had a marvellous run, but by then we weren't sorry to see the end of it, because we had given a hundred performances, and at four hours long it was quite exhausting.

We played *Antony and Cleopatra* in repertoire with *Entertaining Strangers,* a new play by David Edgar, set in the nineteenth century. Tim played the leading part of a vicar, and I was the owner of a brewery. We all went down in a bus to Dorchester, and were shown round the Eldridge Pope brewery. We learnt all about hops and how they brewed the beer.

I had a scene with a baby at the beginning, and I said it would be wonderful to have a real baby, not a doll. It lasted two nights. I said, 'I'm not having that baby, it's joining in.' It was hopeless, I thought it would be such a good idea, but the baby went back. I loved doing the play, but the part was strangely unsatisfying, I found the jumps in it quite difficult. We had a big scene in a churchyard when it started to snow, and it was hugely effective, except that you could see people in the audience tasting it, and I thought, Oh, come *on.*

This was a promenade production in the Lyttelton, and one night I saw the director Howard Davies sitting in the front row, cross-legged, so I wrote a note saying, 'I suppose a screw is out of the question?' and as I went by I dropped it into the lap of the man next to him!

We opened on the night of the Great Storm in 1987. We stayed at Hampstead that night, and the next day Finty and I had to return to the house we had bought in the country not long before. We drove down the lane in a convoy, over power lines that were all down. A huge branch of the oak tree had fallen, and I had a neighbour who worked in wood, so we gave it to him and he carved it into hearts of oak. I gave one to everybody in the cast on the first night of my next play at the National, which was *Hamlet.* But before I embarked on that production I had to give a lot of thought to the one I had promised to direct for Ken Branagh.

Every night at the
Old Vic I watched each
play in the season from
the wings. I learnt so
much from watching
others.

Above: On holiday in France with my brother Jeffery, my sister-in-law Daphne and my father.

Left: With Paul Daneman as Sir Toby Belch and John Neville as Andrew Aguecheek in *Twelfth Night*. I played Maria with a Yorkshire accent, which seemed to fit the character well.

Two early TV roles in 1960:
Princess of France with
Robert Hardy in the BBC
series *The Age of Kings* (*right*);
and a tearaway girl in Z-Cars
(*below*), a character later
developed into Terry in John
Hopkins's *Talking to a Stranger*.

With Franco Zeffirelli
rehearsing *Romeo and Juliet*,
1960. Franco was quite unlike
any other director I ever
worked for.

With Peggy Ashcroft and Dorothy Tutin in *The Cherry Orchard*. Peggy said, 'I have a feeling that you're going to have a hard time. Michel always picks on someone, just don't let him see you cry.'

A dance routine for a charity fundraiser with other actresses at the London Palladium. I'm on the far right.

Above left: I had a brilliant wig made in Paris out of yak hair for *A Midsummer Night's Dream* – it was like the top of a dandelion.

Above right: I enjoyed playing Isabella in *Measure for Measure* though we only had mixed notices for it.

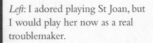

Left: I adored playing St Joan, but I would play her now as a real troublemaker.

In the film of *The Dream* the costumes kept being cut down, until I ended up just being sprayed in green paint every morning.

Sally Bowles in *Cabaret*. The thing I learnt from Hal Prince was that the story doesn't stop for the song, it carries on the story.

Perdita in *The Winter's Tale*, with Roger Rees as Florizel.

Viola in *Twelfth Night* with Donald Sinden, who was quite brilliant as Malvolio.

Our wedding day, 5 February 1971.

Michael rehearsing in my going-away hat.

Above: Trevor Nunn gave us a lovely advance wedding present by casting us as the young lovers in *London Assurance*.

Below: The Merchant of Venice with Michael as Bassanio. I had this idea of a wig for Portia with lots of curls, and John Neville put his head round my dressing-room door and said, 'Hello Bubbles.' That was all he said.

With Finty as a baby.

Michael and Finty on holiday in Cyprus.

Finty in her communion outfit.

Macbeth was the play that Ian McKellen and I most wanted to do, but initially Trevor Nunn was very reluctant.

In *Langrishe, Go Down*, Jeremy Irons was a German student, and I played the uninhibited object of his affections.

Beatrice in rehearsal for *Much Ado About Nothing* with Donald Sinden as Benedick. The director, John Barton, set it at the time of the British Raj in India, which worked brilliantly.

I loved the challenge of doing *Juno and the Paycock* with an all-Irish cast, and it was a great help to have old friends like Norman Rodway there.

With Anna Massey in *A Kind of Alaska*, as the victim of sleeping sickness awakening after sixteen years.

Michael played my husband in *Pack of Lies*, though we never talked about work when we came home.

In *Mr and Mrs Nobody*, which Michael and I mistakenly thought would be an absolute breeze.

Playing Goneril to John Gielgud's King Lear on BBC Radio 3, with an all-star cast.

With Tim Pigott-Smith (left) and Peter Hall (right) on a research trip for *Entertaining Strangers*. Tim started our long-running black glove saga; the gloves are now on display in his study.

With Helen Fitzgerald and Miranda Foster in *Antony and Cleopatra*. Alison Chitty designed the wonderful costumes, with all the Egyptian characters in earth tones of orange, yellow and pink.

Gertrude with Daniel Day-Lewis as Hamlet at the National Theatre, 1989. I thought I would try to play her like his real mother, Jill Balcon, tall and dark, but found I couldn't do it.

With Michael Pennington as my husband in *The Gift of the Gorgon*. It was a great success, and I still don't know why I was the only person not to enjoy that play.

Christine Foskett in *Absolute Hell*, 1995. Still today if anyone asks me what I want to be doing tonight, my answer is *Absolute Hell*.

Left and *below:* Preparing to play Esme in David Hare's *Amy's View,* directed by Richard Eyre (left). David (centre) was a huge comfort throughout the rehearsal period.

Right: With Patricia Hodge rehearsing *A Little Night Music,* which broke all previous box office records at the National.

With Michael at John Mills's eightieth birthday party. We had been friends with Johnny ever since he and I first worked together in *The Good Companions*, and he was a man after my own heart.

Enjoying the garden at home.

Michael learning some bad news for England in the sports report.

Finty with a very alert Sammy.

Michael and Sammy at Eriska.

With Finty, Sammy and Minnie.

With Geoffrey Palmer in *As Time Goes By*. Geoffrey taught me to fine-tune my timing on television.

In *Cranford* with Lisa Dillon, Eileen Atkins and Imelda Staunton.

Pierce Brosnan and I got on very well indeed, and I loved M's line rebuking Bond, calling him 'a sexist, misogynistic dinosaur'.

With a new Bond, Daniel Craig, in *Casino Royale*. He too is hugely good fun to work with, and does most of his stunts himself.

With the writer and director of *Shakespeare in Love*, Tom Stoppard (left) and John Madden, at the announcement of the Oscar nominations.

With the Oscar for Best Supporting Actress. I was so surprised to win it for eight quick minutes with bad teeth.

On the set of *Tea with Mussolini*, when Finty brought Sammy out for his first Italian holiday.

With Kevin Spacey, who played my nephew in *The Shipping News*. He is a brilliant mimic with a good ear for other actors' voices.

Bob Hoskins and I had a terrible time dancing in *Mrs Henderson Presents*. Bob said, 'The trouble with you is you have hooves instead of feet.'

With Toby Stephens in *The Royal Family*. One night during the run he heard he had got the part of the villain in the next Bond film, and then had to say the line onstage, 'Oh God, I hate pictures.'

After a performance of *The Breath of Life* with Maggie Smith and a visiting member of the audience who looked familiar.

Ladies in Lavender, directed by Charles Dance. One critic moaned, 'This film will only appeal to fans of Maggie Smith and Judi Dench.'

With Jim Broadbent in *Iris* in 2001. He won the Oscar for it, and it was very exciting to be there with him that night.

In *Notes on a Scandal*, as the terrifying schoolteacher Barbara Covett, with Cate Blanchett.

Two strongly contrasting films in 2009. *Nine*, a large-scale musical with an international cast; and *Rage*, shot on a shoestring as a series of monologues filmed against a coloured screen.

My first appearance at the BBC Proms in July 2010, in a concert performed to honour Stephen Sondheim on his eightieth birthday.

■ ■ ■ ■

10
DIRECTING FOR THE
FIRST TIME
1985–1993

■ ■ ■ ■

I first worked with Kenneth Branagh in the 1985 BBC Television production of Ibsen's *Ghosts,* when I played Mrs Alving and he was my son Oswald. That is a dark play, but Pastor Manders was played by Michael Gambon, who is a terrible joker, so we had one moment of pure farce. The director Elijah Moshinsky asked us to improvise a scene around the dinner table to run under the credits, as the camera panned across our faces. He said that he would dub in a music track later, over our adlibbed murmur of conversation. This was asking for trouble with Michael.

When Natasha Richardson as the maid offered him some potatoes, and they were very large potatoes, Michael said, 'Yes please, I'll have twelve.' Once the camera had left him he started to corpse, and so did I as soon it passed me, which was too much for Ken, who just collapsed with laughter as the camera reached him. All the attempted retakes were hopeless, so we were sent home in disgrace and had to shoot that scene again the following day. Apart from that hiccup, we all worked very happily together, and it began my long friendship with Ken.

When he invited me to direct a play for his new Renaissance Company in 1988 he asked me which one it should be. There was only a moment's pause before we both said together — *Much Ado About Nothing.* I knew the play well, and had loved playing Beatrice to Donald Sinden's Benedick. For his Beatrice, Ken suggested Samantha Bond. The three of us met in my dressing room at the National, and the casting was quickly agreed.

I didn't ask any of the other actors to do audition speeches, because we were all rather nervous. I was nervous about directing, and I think they were all nervous about me directing them. I thought we would talk, I would put them at their ease, so we would have a cup of tea. I ended up having twenty-five cups of tea or coffee, and doing most of the talking, asking them questions and answering them myself — just to put them at their ease. Some would come in and say, 'Oh, I don't want to sit there, I'll sit on the floor.' Some would come in a kind of disguise, and I longed to say, 'Look, I'm an actor, and I understand that fear.'

My Michael kept asking me about my concept for the play, and I said, 'I have no concept at all, and I don't want one. I don't want to go with a cut-and-dried feeling of what I want.' I thought I would just let my thoughts wash through a sieve as we worked on it. What I was very sure about was that you could not update it too far, because it concerned and worried me that if you do, say, *Romeo and Juliet* in modern dress, then why didn't they just phone Friar Lawrence? So I was always asking questions about the play, and I just wanted to tell the story very clearly. I thought ultimately that it must be set in Messina, it must be in a hot country.

When our designer Jenny Tiramani came to the National to talk to me about it, I told her that I didn't want one of those moments where a young man comes on in tights and you don't actually listen to what he says at first, because you are eyeing him up and down a bit and thinking, Oh, he looks all right in tights. I think there is something very removed about that, which I didn't want. I wished to make the play more accessible, but not to have it played in jeans. So then I thought of setting it in Italy at the time of Shelley, early Victorian, which is very good for the men, and also very good for the women, especially if you have a very sparky Victorian girl, which is also rather unusual.

It took me back to the days when I wanted to be a designer, all those years ago. I never knew why I did that training really, but I have always felt that you perhaps do something which is for the best in the end, even if at the time it may not seem so. When it came to directing I realised that I did see a whole series of pictures in my mind, and that helped me enormously with directing a play.

The other thing I discovered was that the first thing a director has to have is energy. I had always thought that I had a lot of that, but I came home after one long rehearsal in London and sat down in my coat, and the family said, 'Do you want a cup of tea?' 'No, I don't want a cup of tea.' Then a quarter of an hour later, as they were watching the news, I got up and went straight upstairs to bed, where I slept from a quarter to eight that night until a quarter to eight the next morning. You not only have to have the energy to think up things, but you have to watch everybody minutely, with a kind of all-seeing eye. You need to use that as an

192

actor, but as a director you have to use it to the nth degree. I knew from being an actress that if you did something new or different, you were very irritated if it was not noticed in rehearsal.

A friend of mine was told by one of the actors, 'She goes very, very quickly,' because I didn't enjoy blocking the play at all. I am an inveterate list-maker, so I made masses of lists before I started. I did a million drawings about where people should meet, and then of course I didn't do any of that. The other requirement for me in a director, as you may have gathered by now, is that a sense of humour is essential. We did laugh a great deal in rehearsals, and out of humour come so many things, the malleable quality that humour creates in people is of vital importance when you are working with them.

It helps when you have to get over things that you think are serious, notes that you have to give, observations that you have to make; you can often do it with humour, whereas in another context it could be taken as cruelty. I can still remember Michael Langham saying to me all those years before at the Old Vic, when he was directing *The Dream* and I was playing Hermia, 'You come in, with all that energy, and all you throw over to us is like a rubber ball coming on, bouncing all over the stage.' I thought, Oh, how cruel. He was absolutely right, but there are kinder ways of putting it.

The actors' own creativity, and the response to direction from each of them, was remarkable. Whatever I gave out, I got this huge response back from everybody, and I felt that because I had been through my own learning process, in thirty years with Shakespeare, I could actually pass on something that would help them in this play. I was so anxious not to do to Samantha Bond what Michel Saint-Denis had done to me in *The Cherry Orchard,* that I was perhaps over-careful not to give her line-readings. When she asked me if hers was right, I used to say, 'There is another way,' and let her find her own interpretation for herself. I couldn't say to Sam, 'This is how I played it,' and nor would it have been right for her. When she said, 'Kill Claudio,' it got the gasp that it should, where when I played Beatrice it often got the laugh that it shouldn't. So she did succeed in finding her own way.

What I did say to the cast, probably every day, was, 'I want you to go out and tell the story. You must never forget that there is a story here to be told, and that's what our business is. I don't want anyone coming on and doing it on their own, coming on and striking thirteen. I'm not interested in that, I'm interested in somebody coming on and re-creating this story as if it were for the first time.'

We could not afford an arbour for the eavesdropping scene, so Ken used to sit in the middle of four little trees. Patrick Doyle composed the music for 'Sigh No More, Ladies', and he would sing one verse, and Ken would start to go out just as Patrick started to sing again. Ken would go, 'Oh Christ!' I was outraged and said to him, 'You absolutely mustn't say that.' I had to give him a note: 'I don't want to hear "Oh Christ" or "Oh God", I simply don't want to hear it right in the middle of Pat's song.'

Hugh Cruttwell, the former Head of RADA, was a great friend and adviser to Ken Branagh, and he came to the first run-through. I was terribly nervous about him seeing it, and it was all going so well until they came to the scene where they are all in the tomb singing, when they all started to laugh. I was apoplectic with rage, I was absolutely furious with them.

Then of course it all turns back on you, because you think, Oh, I have done that, I have been accused of that. When Peter Hall urged me to direct, he said, 'Go and do it, see how difficult it is.' I began to see what he meant, because I never realised before how transparent actors can be. They come in and try to do something, and then they say, 'Oh, I'm so sorry, I don't know this, I was working at it all night.' They are glassily transparent. You know when they have, and you know when they haven't. Then they all go off to the pub and gang up against you.

Fortunately I had Rachel Kavanaugh as my assistant. She is my godchild and had just finished university, and she turned out to be the most brilliant assistant. Now of course she has turned out to be a very successful director. So having her was a real bonus.

I quite understand that lovely story of when John Gielgud directed *Twelfth Night* at Stratford: before the run-through the actors pleaded, 'Sir John, please, please could we get through it without you interrupting from the stalls. We need to get through it.' He agreed, and Orsino came on and started, 'If music be the food of love —' and Sir John was up out of his seat straight away saying, 'No, no, no, no, no, not like that!' I now know that feeling.

I couldn't but interrupt them when I thought they got it wrong, and yet when they got it right I couldn't but interrupt them again, saying, 'That's exactly how I want you to do it. Do it that way, it's wonderful.' They said, 'Would you just shut up and let us get on with it if that's right.' So I learnt a lot about my behaviour towards a director by being a director, and I learnt not to say, 'I have been up all night looking at this,' unless I really have been.

The production opened at the Birmingham Rep Studio, which holds 150 people, and I had the kind of nerves that I never want to go through again. I have never been so frightened as on that first night at Birmingham, walking round the theatre with Rachel. I had not expected the moment of handing it over to be so painful, that moment of sitting there with an audience in, when you can no longer say, 'Can we stop and do that again?' It was very traumatic indeed.

It was as if the fifteen actors had disappeared, and somebody had come on with a most enormous mirror. There I saw reflected what happens to me at a first performance, that terrifying thing that, if you are not very careful — and I have only experienced a couple of first nights when this hasn't happened to me at one point — you simply withdraw behind a kind of barrier in yourself.

Their nerves made them mis-time some lines, which consequently failed to get the laughs we expected. I was so wound up by this that I couldn't stop myself going round and exploding, 'What are you all doing? It's like watching a multi-car pile-up on the M1!' They took it very well, and when the rest had gone I said to my leading man, 'Oh, Kenny, it was like giving birth to a baby that isn't breathing properly. You watch it trying to walk, and then it falls over and can't get up, and you can't do anything, it's agony.'

As soon as I got back to my room in Birmingham, because of the way it had gone, I then mistrusted entirely my sense of humour. I doubted my own judgement about the play, and that was completely shattering, because I thought, Well, maybe the things that make me laugh don't make other people laugh, maybe we haven't set about telling the story properly, and maybe the decisions that ultimately I had to make were not the right decisions.

So I had a night of real self-analysis about it, but for a bit of that night I slept soundly, and in that sound bit of sleep I recharged my batteries, having made a lot of lists as well, so I was able to ring Michael next day and say, 'Don't come up, I'm all right.' Then I went in and we did probably one of the best day's work for all of us. At the second preview everything clicked, and I was so glad that Frank Hauser chose to come that night.

The day of the press night coincided with my going to Buckingham Palace to receive my DBE. I was the only dame that day, and I was shown into a room with the men who were to be knighted. They have to kneel, but the dames don't. We rehearsed it, and one man said, 'May I smoke?' 'No, but you may play the piano.' The orchestra played 'Half a Sixpence' when I walked up. The most wonderful moment for me came when the Queen was giving awards to those who had saved lives at the Zeebrugge ferry disaster, and I can see them now — a young sailor in bell-bottoms with bright red hair, that man who made the human bridge, and several nuns. It was all terribly moving, and I was glad to be there that day.

Then Michael and I caught the train up to Birmingham. The cast made me promise to wear the same clothes I had worn for the investiture, and they wanted to see the insignia. I lent it to Richard Clifford to wear that night as Don Pedro, and it looked very striking, but I told him very firmly that it was for that one night only.

Before we started rehearsals I said in my innocence, 'What's going to be wonderful about directing is going home in the evening, and doing just what I want.' In fact it isn't like that at all. You go home in the evening, and at five minutes to seven you look at the clock and think, This is the half, I wonder are they feeling like it tonight? and then you look again at half-past seven and think, They are going on now, and have they got this right and that right? Oh, I bet that's getting sloppy. I pored over the show reports, I watched the timing, I looked at all the remarks at the end, and then I went up like a Tartar with my notes and shouted at them. I did let them have a bit of free rein, but the Studio at Birmingham was such a small space that they couldn't have much physical free rein. They could have mental free rein, as long as they didn't push the text out of true.

What I was most concerned about was showing to an audience of tomorrow that reading Shakespeare need not necessarily put you off for life. I had a lot of letters from schoolchildren, and from their teachers who took them to *Much Ado,* who said, 'The story is so clear, and it's helped us enormously, and I really found it both funny and very, very sad.' I thought that was the greatest compliment, and underlines why I think the theatre is important — to make that audience of tomorrow want to go and see more Shakespeare done.

The thing I try and tell myself on the nights I don't feel like performing anything is that the audience has made the effort of going and getting the tickets, they have finished work, have cleaned up somewhere, have come to the theatre; their gesture is the first, and yours must be the second, it is a gift you must return. Of course it isn't always as easy as that. There was one occasion in *The Comedy of Errors* when I didn't feel like it, so I thought, I know what I will do, I will just play the whole thing to somebody. I knew nobody there that night, so I saw a lady in a green coat, and I thought, I'm going to do it entirely for her. So I did it absolutely a hundredfold to her, and told everybody that was who I was doing it for, and when I came back after the interval she had left. So that is where it is dangerous.

After the first night of *Much Ado* I left it for quite a long time, partly because I had the 'flu, and then I went up again to see the production. It had grown in confidence, it had grown alongside an audience, and I saw that the audience and the production had been working together, sometimes to the detriment of the play. I thought that the audience had wooed my company into doing something very, very naughty here. But it is difficult in a comedy, because if you get a huge laugh on something, the next night you want the same laugh or even more, you can't help it because you are hungry for that. But then you have to ask yourself: What is the story here? Perhaps I shouldn't have such a big laugh on that line.

I went back to see my cast at Brighton after they had been touring for three months, and I told them, 'You've all gone very West End, playing it all straight out front.' But none of them were terribly keen on getting my reactions after all that time on their own. Once, when Ken heard that I was in, by the time I got backstage he had left the theatre in his costume to avoid having to hear any of my notes.

He must have quickly forgiven me, because immediately afterwards he asked me to play Mistress Quickly in his film of *Henry V.* So now the roles were reversed, with him directing me. He was also playing the title role, which provoked some very unfair criticisms in the press that he was presuming to challenge Laurence Olivier's famous wartime version. But I couldn't resist ribbing him about his first appearance as the King, as two huge doors swung back to reveal him stamping in: 'I've never seen anyone give themselves such an outrageous entrance!'

The following year Ken asked me to direct him as Jimmy Porter in *Look Back in Anger,* with his wife Emma Thompson as Alison. This was for his own Renaissance production company, put on for just one week in Belfast, to raise funds for charities in Northern Ireland, plus a single Sunday night performance at the London Coliseum in aid of Friends of the Earth. We only had two weeks' rehearsal, which was very short. It was then televised, with just a week to rehearse that, but I did have the very great help of David Jones, who was in control of the camera direction. We sat together in the control room, and David always let me decide which take was best from the actors' point of view.

The same year I went back to my roots at the Central School to direct the students in *Macbeth,* another play with fond memories for me. I thought that was the end of it for me as a director, but then in 1991 Ian Talbot invited me to direct something at the Regent's Park Open-Air Theatre. I had loved playing in *The Comedy of Errors* at the

RSC, and also loved the Rodgers and Hart musical based on it, *The Boys from Syracuse,* so I chose that. On the opening night we had several showers of rain, which stopped the play three times, but the hardy English audience just sat tight under their umbrellas until we began again.

I went back there two years later to direct *Romeo and Juliet,* but that was a much less happy experience. At the same time I was acting every night in Peter Shaffer's *The Gift of the Gorgon,* and therefore had to leave rehearsals every day at 4 p.m. to prepare, so I fear that I didn't really have enough time to spend with my actors, especially the young lovers, Zubin Varla and Rebecca Callard. I had the worst press for anything I directed, and it has proved to be the last. Five productions were enough for me, and I have lost the desire to do any more.

However, looking back on those experiences now, I would say that the pleasures of directing, and being with each of those groups of people, actually did outweigh the unexpected unpleasantness of suddenly being left on the outside, and the door being shut in my face. In retrospect, I did find it attractive to do, and I learnt a lot about the relationships between actors and directors, so I am glad that I was persuaded by Ken Branagh and Peter Hall to give it a try.

11
A RUN OF TRAGEDIES
1989–1992

I had such happy experiences at the National Theatre with Peter Hall that when Richard Eyre took over from him as Director in 1989 and asked me to play Gertrude in his opening production of *Hamlet* I jumped at it. I hoped it might erase the memory of my difficult times as Ophelia thirty years before at the Old Vic, but it was not to be.

Daniel Day-Lewis was cast as Hamlet, and I thought that I would try and play Gertrude like his real mother, the actress Jill Balcon, tall and dark, but found I couldn't do it. David Burke was the Ghost of Hamlet's father, and however hard I tried, I couldn't believe that he and I could have produced Dan. It was also difficult for me not to try and echo Coral Browne, who had been so magical in the part in 1957. Richard Eyre was simultaneously grappling for the first time with all the administrative demands of running the National, with its three theatres, and both of us had some tricky moments with John Castle who was playing Claudius.

Dan had his own identity crisis which overwhelmed him a little way into the run. He had suffered the loss of his real father, the Poet Laureate Cecil Day-Lewis, and one night in the dramatic meeting with the Ghost of Hamlet's father the two bereavements merged for him, he just seized up and could not carry on. Michael Bryant came to make his first entrance as Polonius, and found Dan crying uncontrollably in the wings. While he took him back to his dressing room I went to find Jeremy Northam, our Laertes but also Hamlet's understudy. He went as white as a sheet, but he changed costumes and finished that performance. He did several more until Dan recovered enough to return to the part, which he did when we took the production to Dubrovnik, though even that was not without its extra drama. At the moment when he banged his head against the wall he momentarily forgot that at Fort Lovrjenac it was made of stone, not the wooden scenery of the Olivier.

I had played Ophelia here on the Old Vic European tour, and I was both surprised and touched to find a Yugoslav television crew following me around at the first-night party, so at least someone had remembered that earlier performance. I took some beautiful photographs of a helicopter lowering the gigantic statue of Hamlet's father into the castle at Dubrovnik.

Returning to this particular play in a different part had its problems, but curiously I was made a similar offer during the run at the National. Sam Mendes came to see me and asked me if I would play Madame Ranevsky in *The Cherry Orchard,* the part in which Peggy Ashcroft was so wonderful at the RSC when I was Anya. Peggy was always in my mind when I played it for Sam, as she had been when I did it on television for Richard Eyre in 1980.

Sam was only twenty-three, but he had just had a great success directing Gorky's *Summerfolk* at Chichester, and was very sure of himself. I heard much later that he said he was nervous about directing me, but he certainly never showed any of that at the time. I said to him once in rehearsal, 'I'm not going to do that, I'm going to try something else,' and he said, 'Well, you can if you want, but it won't work,' and he turned his back and refused to watch.

It was in one of my favourite London theatres, the Aldwych, where I had first appeared in the play for the RSC, so I was particularly thrilled to get a note wishing me luck from John Gielgud, who had played Gaev in that production: 'To my favourite actress in my favourite play.' He was such a dear man, with the most exquisite manners.

We had a brilliant new translation by Michael Frayn, and a great cast, including Ronald Pickup as Gaev, Nicholas Farrell as Trofimov, and Michael Gough as the ancient retainer, Firs. Michael gave a radio interview one morning, in which he said, 'I am working with three of the most attractive women in the West End.' I heard this, so when Michael arrived that evening, I rounded up Miranda Foster, Lesley Manville, Abigail McKern and Kate Duchene, and all five of us stood in front of him. I said, 'OK, Michael, who are the three?' He was very cross with us, but that wasn't the only time he was forgetful.

One night he couldn't remember Gaev's full name, and substituted the only Russian name he could think of, and said, 'Vladimir Ashkenazy is out without his coat again.' So I offered a prize to anyone else who could slip other Russian names into their lines, and someone even managed to sneeze making a sound like 'Shos*TAK*ovich.' But I was very fond of Michael, and I wish we had worked together more.

My next play was also directed by Sam: Sean O'Casey's *The Plough and the Stars* at the Young Vic. Dearbhla Molloy had played my daughter in *Juno and the Paycock,* and she talked me into taking the role of Bessie Burgess by saying it was not a very big part, but that all the great Irish actresses had played it, and she had a great death scene. That clinched it for me, but the moment when she is shot is a very difficult scene to get right, and I kept putting off rehearsing it, until about four days before the end of rehearsals, when Sam started to say, 'Look, Judi . . .' Then I said, 'Fine, I'm ready to do it now.' The most vivid note he gave me was passed on from a man who had actually been shot. He said it was like being run through with a red-hot poker, and simultaneously being kicked by a horse with a force that knocked him off his feet. Try playing that effect on stage and making it look convincing.

But I must have got Bessie's appearance right, as one critic described me as 'a blotchy-featured boozer' and another as a 'tottering, brawling rag bag of twitching rage at her lot'. I was both amused and pleased when I was waiting behind a flat to go on after the interval, and overheard one woman say to her friend, 'She played Juliet once,' and got the reply, 'You are *joking!*'

The grief explored in that play was sadly matched in life when I lost one of my dearest friends, Peggy Ashcroft. She had a stroke in May 1991 and was taken to the Royal Free Hospital in Hampstead, where she never regained consciousness. When I went to see her there on 14 June, the Registrar took me into a room and said quietly, 'She died about twenty minutes ago.' I was so glad that I heard the news that way. When I announced it at the end of the performance that night, I thought I wouldn't call for silence, because Peggy wouldn't have wanted that. So I called for applause, and it just went on and on. We could have stood there for half an hour while everyone clapped. She was much loved by audiences, and even more by those of us who had the joy of working with her, and who treasured her friendship. She was such a model for me, from *The Cherry Orchard* on, and she worked right up to the end, giving her last performance on BBC Radio 3 just a month before her stroke, as Mrs Swan in Tom Stoppard's play *In the Native State.* It has always been my expressed intention to do the same.

At her Memorial Service in Westminster

Abbey, Dorothy Tutin and I shared the reading of the dirge from *Cymbeline:* 'Fear no more the heat o' the sun', which is read at many actors' memorials, but it had a special poignancy here, as Peggy had been such a memorable Imogen in that play. Many of us had a lump in our throats as John Gielgud, her great stage partner for half a century, quoted Shakespeare's epitaph for Cleopatra as 'a lass unparallel'd'. The service was televised by the BBC, in recognition of her acknowledged leadership in the theatre. I still miss her.

When *The Plough and the Stars* ended at the Young Vic I found myself working with the same director for the third time in a row, but this time at the National Theatre, where Sam Mendes had been invited to direct Edward Bond's new play *The Sea.* Perhaps Sam asked me to play the monstrous Mrs Rafi because she was described as an East Anglian Lady Bracknell. It was a glorious part to play, and she got more monstrous as the run went on. There was a scene with some amateur theatricals where I was required to over-act outrageously, which I found quite hard to do at first. At the first read-through we couldn't finish that scene, because everybody just collapsed with laughter.

There wasn't so much laughter when we heard that the author was coming to a rehearsal. None of us had met him before, and all the cast were terrified. Edward Bond's earlier plays, like *Saved* and his version of *Lear,* had scenes of great savagery and we didn't quite know what to expect. We got back after lunch to find that he had arrived without us knowing. When the actors came bowling through the door and suddenly saw Edward Bond, they immediately went over into a corner. I glanced at all of them huddled there, looking down and not at each other, and thought that they were behaving exactly like the sheep in a shedding-ring. But he turned out to be a lovely man, and not at all frightening.

Soon after, Kenneth Branagh invited me to play his mother again in *Coriolanus* at Chichester, and I said yes immediately. Volumnia is another rather monstrous character, who is instrumental in destroying her son at the end. The rest of the cast included Iain Glen as Aufidius, Richard Briers as Menenius, and Susannah Harker as Virgilia, with a lot of local amateurs in Chichester recruited to make up the warring armies. One night the major casualty was me.

I came in for the first scene, and there was Susie Harker sitting sewing, I took one step and went straight over on my ankle. When I tried to get up I couldn't. Susie carried on sewing, so I thought there was no help coming from that direction. Ken came rushing on to help me off, and they asked if there was a doctor in the house. Luckily there was, and he told me I had sprained my ankle. He strapped it up, and after a quarter of an hour's delay, I went back on and finished the performance with a stick. But I found it very difficult to walk, so when we all lined up for the curtain call and Susie Harker said, 'I'll take you by the arm for your call,' I said, 'I wish you would.'

We were the penultimate call, with Ken coming on after us, but that night he just ran on before us, took his call, and then did an enormous flourish towards us as I came on. I was rather overcome by the ovation which greeted me. Ken must have sensed that, because after we all bowed three times and turned to leave, he hissed at me, 'Get off the stage, you limping bitch,' which certainly defused the emotion.

When the run ended at Chichester, I went back to the RSC for a new play by Peter Shaffer at the Barbican. I was a great admirer of his work, both *Five Finger Exercise* and *Royal Hunt of the Sun* had made a great impression on me, and at this time I was doing a radio play of his, *Whom Do I Have the Honour of Addressing?* But if I had read *The Gift of the Gorgon* to the end I would never have agreed to do it.

My part was the widow of a playwright, Edward Damson, who is visited on a Greek island by his illegitimate son Philip, played by Jeremy Northam, who wants to write the biography of the father he never met. Much of the story was told in flashback, and my husband was played by Michael Pennington. Peter Hall was directing, so all the omens were good, but I just couldn't get to grips with the play. At one rehearsal I was in such despair that I threw the script away and locked myself in the loo. Peter spent a long time persuading me to carry on, which I eventually did reluctantly.

We did it in the tiny Pit Theatre in the Barbican, a building I hate, and I told the RSC directors Adrian Noble and Michael Attenborough so, when they came round on the last night. I said I would never go back there to do a play, whatever the circumstances. I think it is a monstrous building, and we have no business to be there. You never see the company, because you are all in those awful cells. I had a room which looked out on to the underground car park, full of fumes, with dirty windows.

There is no positive way you can run a theatre company there successfully, always going up and down in lifts, with nowhere to meet the other actors.

Despite all my own misgivings, the play was such a great success with both the press and the public that it transferred to Wyndham's Theatre in the West End, where it also sold out. I tried hard not to transfer with it, but finally gave in when Peter Hall rang me and said, 'Look, Judi, are you really prepared to put all these other people out of work?' So we played for another six months to packed houses, but then I did put my foot down, and refused to extend it any further. After all this time, I still don't know why I was the only person not to enjoy that play. Finty came to it and was so wiped out at the end of it that she couldn't bring herself to come round afterwards.

What helped my equilibrium through this seemingly unending sequence of tragedies on the stage was beginning work on my second television sitcom, which eventually ran from 1991 for more than a decade.

■ ■ ■ ■

12
WORKING IN
TELEVISION
1978–2002

■ ■ ■ ■

Today many young actors see their careers in terms of TV or the cinema, with the occasional time out for a short run of something in the theatre. In my early years it was the complete opposite — most of my work was in the theatre, but then my generation was lucky enough to have all those flourishing repertory theatres. So I did only the very occasional screen work. We will come to my late entry into films in another chapter, and my television credits before I was offered the sitcoms were also few and far between, apart from *Talking to a Stranger*. Two of them were recordings of RSC productions anyway — *The Comedy of Errors* and *Macbeth* — made by Thames Television for ITV. Three others I remember particularly, for different reasons — *Langrishe, Go Down* for the BBC, and *Love in a Cold Climate* and *Saigon — Year of the Cat,* both for Thames.

Langrishe, Go Down was based on a novel

by Aidan Higgins, adapted by Harold Pinter, and directed by David Jones. Set in Ireland just before the Second World War, it told the story of three sisters; Annette Crosbie was one of the others, and my character had an affair with a German student, played by Jeremy Irons. I was the very uninhibited object of his affections, with several nude scenes to play. David came down to talk these through with both Michael and me, to explain why they were integral to the plot.

This girl used to take air baths, and I had to run across a meadow with absolutely no clothes on. They said to me, 'It's fine, because you can keep your wig and your earrings on.' 'Well, thanks a lot, that's a great, great comfort.' The camera was right up a tree, and I ran across this meadow, where my dresser Lizzie Scamp was waiting behind a bush. She said, 'You look like a lovely birthday card,' so I didn't mind doing it then. I also had to be nude in a river, and in bed with Jeremy.

We stayed in the Hotel Waterford, which had a great long neon sign at the side, and when it lit up at night we expected it to say Hotel Waterford, but instead it said Hotel Inexpensive, which amused us all no end. I had to fly back to London for a recital on the first weekend, and nobody had yet seen the rushes. So I said, 'If when I come back there is a towel hanging out of a window, I'll know that the rushes are all right and I can come in.' There was a towel hanging out of a window, so I was very relieved.

Finty was only six years old when this was made, so I forbade her to watch it then. It was re-shown in New York not so long ago, and then I read in the paper that I didn't want it to be screened again here. I had made no comment whatsoever about it, so I don't know who thought they spoke on my behalf.

There was no risk of any nude scenes in *Love in a Cold Climate.* Simon Raven adapted Nancy Mitford's novel, and we all wore beautiful Thirties costumes. A bonus for me was that Michael was also in the cast, with old friends like John Moffatt and Job Stewart. Donald McWhinnie was the director, and it must have been a nightmare for him to schedule, as it was shot during the ITV technicians' work-to-rule in 1979, meaning that our first call on location was not until 11 a.m., and we had to wrap at 4 p.m. so that the crew could travel in normal working hours. For the actors it meant that we were left at the hotel enjoying long evenings and great meals; we had such a good time, which I recall with great pleasure when I am called for 6 a.m. so often these days.

It was also the shortest rehearsal time I have ever known. I remember rehearsing a scene once with John Moffatt, and Donald just shrugged and said, 'Fine, finished for the day.' Moff and I left the room looking at our watches, saying, 'Seven minutes, that's a pretty good rehearsal time.' Whenever we asked, 'Donald, don't you want to do it again?' he just replied, 'No, I don't want you to get stale. I've cast it perfectly, why bother to go on?'

He had too, with the cast including Michael Aldridge, Jean-Pierre Cassel, Patience Collier, Adrienne Corri, Lucy Gutteridge, and Vivian Pickles. The locations were where the Mitford family had lived, and many of the characters were based on real people. Not surprisingly, the locals used to come and watch the filming, taking an exceptional interest in what we were doing. One rather grand lady asked me, 'And who are you?' I said I was playing Sadie, Lady Alconleigh. 'Oh yes, I knew her very well. She was very, very tall, and very, very pretty.' She paused, and looked at me, and then added, 'But I suppose you'll do it with acting.' I got much taller from then on.

We had to travel from one place in Warwickshire to another location about five miles away, so three of us were driven there in a huge vintage Daimler by a uniformed chauffeur. We were sitting in the back in our cloche hats, without a camera in sight. It was as if we had all suddenly gone back in time. We had the most glorious ten months working on it, and when the union went on strike in the middle of it we were all kept on retainers. I am not at all sure that would happen today, in a very different TV era.

The series was a great success abroad as well as here, and it tickled my sense of humour that the very first country to buy *Love in a Cold Climate* was Iceland. I do hope they knew what they were getting.

Everything I made for television up until then was set in this country, so I was initially thrilled to be offered *Saigon — Year of the Cat*. David Hare had written the script about the final days of the American evacuation of the city, and Stephen Frears was the director. Again the production company was Thames Television, who were still struggling with their union problems. So poor Stephen had even more trouble with the filming schedule in Thailand than Donald had had in England, as the daily rosters were organised from London, not Bangkok.

I was playing Barbara, an English bank

clerk who has an affair with an American CIA agent, played by Frederic Forrest. Unfortunately, Freddy had worked with Marlon Brando on another Vietnam movie — *Apocalypse Now*. Brando told him to improvise his lines rather than say those that were in the script. David and Stephen went wild, but they tried being very diplomatic about it. It didn't help that Freddy was also very angry about the whole business of America being blamed for the Vietnam War.

There were problems with the helicopters provided by the Thai Army for the evacuation at the end, and the day before we shot it there was a huge disaster between two Chinooks on that same airfield. So Stephen hid the newspapers from me, though in fact I would have drawn comfort from that, thinking that if it is going to happen one day, it won't happen the next, will it?

Eventually, the union situation made it impossible to carry on shooting in Bangkok. I was beginning to get homesick, and all the delays made me miss Finty even more, so David and Stephen arranged to fly her and Michael out for the last couple of weeks. She was already a good swimmer at the age of ten, so she was in her element, and it was in Thailand that she learnt to dive. She swam with Clarke Peters, who was in the film, and she has never forgotten that he couldn't float. We were all in this huge swimming pool, he would lie on the top and simply go straight down and lie on the bottom.

Then they stopped the filming, and nine months later we finished it back at Shepperton Studios and Battersea Park. We had all lost our tropical tans by then, so had to spend some time on sunbeds to get them back. It was very cold when we shot the bedroom scenes, and we had to be sprayed with water to make us look sweaty and hot and tropical. David Hare said that it was the most nightmarish shoot he had ever experienced, and it was a miracle that the finished film worked as well as it did.

All of my decisions about work are based on who I am going to work with — actors, writers or directors. The main reason I accepted the offer of Jean in the TV series *As Time Goes By* was so that I could work with Geoffrey Palmer, because there is nobody with a drier sense of comedy, he is a real master. He never even trained at drama school, he went into the Marines. Do the Marines teach you to be a very good comedy actor? Perhaps they should put that on their recruiting posters: 'Join the Marines and become a very, very good comedy actor.'

When we had met briefly a couple of times before this, we had not got off to a very good start. The first time was one Christmas, when I was in the General Trading Company in Chelsea with Finty, and I thought he was trying to pick me up. He said loudly, 'I'd rather be anywhere in the world than here.' He told me later that he nearly didn't say hello in case I did think he was trying to pick me up.

The second time was worse. Tenniel Evans had been a friend since we were together in the York Cycle of Mystery Plays, and he was now thinking of becoming a lay priest. Geoffrey said to Tenniel, 'Rubbish, you mustn't do that.' When Michael and I went to see *An Evening with Peter Ustinov* we found ourselves sitting right in front of the Palmers, so I turned round and said, 'I hear what you've done to Tenniel Evans, how dare you!'

But I couldn't resist the opportunity to work with him, and this sitcom was also written by Bob Larbey, who had written *A Fine Romance,* so I knew we were in good hands. This was the first time I worked with Syd Lotterby, but I knew he had directed such comedy classics as *Porridge, Open All Hours,* and *Yes, Minister.* Syd and Geoffrey took me out to lunch to talk about it, but what I didn't know then was that Jean Simmons had been their first choice, until she decided to do a TV series in America instead. It was years later that that story finally leaked out, and I gave Geoffrey a hard time then for keeping it secret so long. This sitcom was a different kind of romance, between a nurse and a soldier who lose touch when he goes off to the Korean War. They marry other people, and meet by chance thirty-five years later when she is widowed and he is divorced. The mutual attraction is rekindled, and eventually they get married.

We got on very well, perhaps because we each prepared so differently. He used to read all the scripts for the entire series before we started on the first episode, while I arrived for the first read-through not even having read that one. I obviously have a terrible fear of doing so. There is something about the whole business of reading it in advance, and discovering that there is a particular jump you have to clear. Unlike those jockeys who walk around Becher's Brook before the Grand National, I would think, Well, I'll know how high it is when I come to it. I wouldn't be a careful jockey.

As a result we had to learn each episode's

script very quickly. The first read-through was on Tuesdays, and we had to be word-perfect by Friday for the run-through with all the camera crew. Saturday morning we had two fast run-throughs before I usually had to go off to do a matinee in the theatre, and camera rehearsal began at 10.30 a.m. on the Sunday, with the recording before a studio audience at 8 p.m. Monday was our one day off, then we started all over again on the next episode.

Geoffrey taught me to fine-tune my timing on television. He thinks I do too much, and I try not to, but sometimes I can't resist another look, or another double-take. I am always rather nervous when he comes to see me in a play, because he speaks his mind very much, and I quite like that. What both of us did from quite early on in the rehearsals for *As Time Goes By* was to say, 'Oh, we don't need this line, I can get the laugh with just a look.' Usually we did, too, but in situation comedy you sometimes get a very unexpected laugh that you didn't think was there. Sometimes you don't get one which you know is there, and that is even more irritating, because your timing goes completely out of the window. So to be really good at situation comedy is to be really skilled, like Geoffrey. With the other members of the regular cast — Moira Brooker, Jenny Funnell, Philip Bretherton, Moyra Fraser and Paul Chapman — we really were like a happy family.

Syd was a tower of strength too, he used to laugh and laugh so much, and that was really encouraging. Then at the Sunday night recording he would be flying up and down the stairs to the control room. When we had to come out and meet the studio audience he never liked us to say, 'and behind you in the box is the wonderful Syd Lotterby', he never liked us to say anything like that, but we did.

We all thought it would probably run for just one series, but that first one in 1991 had an audience of twelve million, so series two was immediately commissioned. At the end of every subsequent series we all thought it would be the last, but we finally did nine series from 1991 to 2002 before calling it a day. Even then, that was not quite the end, as the BBC asked us to come back for a couple of specials for showing over Christmas a few years later.

It proved hugely popular in America and Australia, and still is; I think they rerun the nine series in an almost continuous loop. Once, a great big parcel arrived at the studio with a message from a lady who said, 'Jean would never have that quilt on her bed, here is the one she would have.' I quite like them feeling that they knew us all so well as those characters, even if sometimes they thought that Geoffrey was my real husband. In America there is an *As Time Goes By* Internet Fan Club, and a whole group of them flew over in 2001 to see *The Royal Family* when I was playing that on the stage in London. What was both surprising and heart-warming about that visit was that they came in the aftermath of the terrible attacks on the Twin Towers in New York, when so many Americans stopped flying anywhere abroad for a while.

The only nasty thing that happened to me during all those years of making *As Time Goes By* was at the Press Call for the first series. A woman journalist had the extraordinary nerve to ask me: 'Who was the first person you slept with, and where was that?' I couldn't believe my ears. I vowed I would never expose myself again to such offensive questioning, and nor have I.

■ ■ ■ ■

13
FROM *THE SEAGULL*
TO *A LITTLE NIGHT*
MUSIC
1993–1995

■ ■ ■ ■

1993 was not my happiest year. I finally stepped off what had become for me the treadmill of *The Gift of the Gorgon,* and I had an even more upsetting experience in my family life before the year was out. It happened during what was otherwise a wonderfully fulfilling experience — Radio 3's celebration of John Gielgud's ninetieth birthday with an all-star production of *King Lear.* This was transmitted on his actual birthday, 14 April 1994, but because of the logistics of gathering that supporting cast, it was recorded the previous September. Ken Branagh had proposed this as a Renaissance co-production with the BBC, and he played Edmund. I was cast as Goneril, and the rest of the cast list read like a Who's Who in British Theatre, with even the tiny part of the Herald played by Peter Hall.

We recorded it over a week, and the night before the final studio day I drove home to

Surrey. Finty was now living in our old Hampstead house with a couple of friends, and she was woken by the smell of smoke. A burning candle had set fire to the curtains, so she called the fire brigade, who were there until 4 a.m. Fortunately the girls decided to sleep downstairs, because the fire blazed up again a couple of hours later, and virtually gutted the house this time before it was put out. I rushed up there as fast as I could in the morning, and in my relief that no one was hurt, and my distress at seeing the burnt-out shell of our first married home, I just burst into tears.

I rang Glyn Dearman, who was directing *King Lear,* to say I would now be a bit late for the recording, but I would be OK to do it so long as no one mentioned the fire. He managed to warn everyone except Sir John, who rushed up to me as soon as he came into the studio and burst out, 'Oh, Judi, my poor darling, are you insured?' His concern was just too much for me, and I broke down, sobbing on his shoulder. I lost a lot of precious theatre mementoes in the fire, but then Sir John, with his usual thoughtful generosity, sent me a little box that Peggy Ashcroft had given him, to help replace them. The fire overshadowed the end of what had been a lovely week, although our star himself, self-critical as ever, wished we had had more rehearsal time to get it better.

After that difficult year it was very good to go back to the National Theatre, which turned out to be my stage home for the next five years. The first production was of *The Seagull,* directed by John Caird, whom I had known at Stratford, though we had never worked together before. He wanted to stage it in the Cottesloe, but Richard Eyre insisted that it had to be in the Olivier.

I love Chekhov, but Arkadina is a hard part to play. She behaves so appallingly, she is the most terrible mother that anyone has ever written. In the middle scene, when she woos Trigorin, I used to get Bill Nighy lying on the ground under me, and after every line of mine he used to say under his breath, 'Oh, my God,' which I am sure is exactly what Trigorin was feeling.

If there were ever the slightest risk of my taking myself, or a particular part, too seriously, I can always rely on my friends to send me up, and I still treasure a poem I received from John Moffatt during the rehearsals for this play:

Dame Judi Dench . . . known as Jude
Was excessively vulgar and lewd.

If she got no applause
She would shout 'Up Yours!'
To the audience. Dreadfully rude!

From the first act right through to the last
She'd insult the rest of the cast.
She would sometimes yell 'Balls!'
To the orchestra stalls
And leave *ev'ryone* simply aghast.

The director said sadly 'Oh, dear,
Dame Judi's too vulgar I fear.
For the lead in *The Seagull*
I'd have liked Anna Neagle.
What a pity she's no longer here.

Next at the National was one of my very
favourite plays, *Absolute Hell* by Rodney
Ackland. This was partly at my instigation,
as I had played Christine Foskett in the
television production in 1991. It is based
on a real Soho club, re-named La Vie en
Rose, and is about the life of all these
extraordinary bohemian people there at the
end of the war. There was all the sleaziness
of such a place, but the characters were
touching and interesting. In those less
permissive times of the early Fifties, when it
was first staged in London, the critics
panned it for its lack of morals, and it was

taken off very quickly, to the great distress of its author.

Anthony Page persuaded the BBC to televise it in a rewritten version, and asked me to play the club owner, who was also based on a real person. By now Rodney Ackland was old and frail, but he came to the studio recording in a wheelchair, and watching it he was moved to tears. I was saddened by his reaction, until he said to me, 'I didn't realise I had written such a good play.' I had a wonderful drunk scene towards the end, and the whole thing was such fun to do, that I said to Anthony afterwards, 'Wouldn't it be lovely to do this in the theatre?' Three years later we did, with a number of changes to the cast. Bill Nighy had played Hugh Marriner, a failed writer, on TV, now Greg Hicks took the part on stage, and my old friend from our school-days, Peter Woodthorpe, was the terrible and overbearing film director Maurice Hussey.

I thought I had made Christine too genteel on TV, so I made her much coarser on stage, and more drunk. In fact, although we were of course only drinking coloured water, I used to feel absolutely stocious afterwards. I can remember one night saying to Greg Hicks as we were on our hands and knees, 'How can we both be so drunk on coloured water?' There was a whole atmosphere about that play that was quite heady, and there were great rewards in it, because although parts of it are very sad, other parts are very, very funny.

The set at the Lyttelton was the bar of this club, with some stairs up the side, and you couldn't get out the back, it was all contained very nicely in this set. So when we disappeared behind the back to serve somebody, you couldn't get out.

I was only sad that Rodney Ackland didn't live to see his play as praised by the theatre critics as it had been by the TV critics, even if there were some remarks about 'a flawed masterpiece'. It could have run for much longer, but the Lyttelton was needed for the next shows. It is still the play that if anyone asks me what I want to be doing tonight, my answer is *Absolute Hell.*

Happily, my next appearance at the National was also very rewarding. I had always admired the songs in *A Little Night Music,* so I was thrilled when Richard Eyre asked me to play Desirée Armfeldt. The role of my mother was played by Siân Phillips; she is only a year or so older than me, but that didn't trouble her a bit. 'We'll do it all with wigs,' she said. In fact she had asked the director, Sean Mathias, if she could play that part before she knew who was to play Desirée, because she was as mad about Stephen Sondheim's score as I was. I would have to take something from it to my Desert Island, if the BBC ever asked me to do *Desert Island Discs* again.

I was glad that Siân had worked with Sean before, as I became a bit worried in rehearsals when we spent so long doing exercises with bamboo sticks, instead of working on the script. Siân kept telling me it would be all right, and I trusted her judgement.

The American actor Larry Guittard played my ex-lover, Fredrik Egerman; we only met on the first day of rehearsal, but quickly became terrific friends. To begin with, I kept falling over, in his number 'You must meet my wife'; he'd turn the other way and I'd fall over. He'd turn back and think, Oh, good grief — where is she? I was just lying on the ground.

Stephen Sondheim was in London during the rehearsal period, and kept asking to come and see it, but Sean insisted on putting him off until he had sorted out the technical problems. We had another revolving stage, but thank goodness they seemed to have improved the technology since our troubles over *Mother Courage.* When Stephen eventually came to a preview, I was not sure whether he liked it, but I think he enjoyed it more at a later one. I asked him for a note on the 'Send in the Clowns' song, but he charmingly declined, saying, 'No, that's yours now,' which was most encouraging.

The best moment in rehearsing a musical is when the band arrive, after weeks with only a piano accompaniment. I first realised that when I did *Cabaret* in 1968. I was sitting in Julian Belfrage's garden, and that clever actor David Hutcheson asked me how far we were into rehearsal. I said about six weeks, and he said, 'Wait till the band call.' That is electrifying. You are standing there at the beginning, and then you hear the orchestra start up, and it is like an enormous kind of cushion that you are on. It is wonderful, because you are suddenly lifted up with it. It is even more thrilling if you can be absolutely sure of the notes you are singing, but it is still thrilling if you are not.

A Little Night Music ran for a whole year in the repertoire, and then we came back for an eight-week run in the Olivier, giving eight performances a week. We played to packed houses, and it broke all previous box office records at the National, so everyone was happy. On New Year's Eve, I turned upstage to Larry Guittard and opened my dressing gown to show him 'Happy New Year' written on my corset. On the very last night we were all very sad, so when I opened my dressing gown to Larry this time I had written 'Go home, Yank', just to cheer him up. I only meant him to see it, but had forgotten that the upstage band also had a very clear view.

We threw an end-of-show party with a late-night cabaret for friends in the other National Theatre companies. I dressed up in a dirndl skirt and flaxen plaits to sing a send-up of 'Sixteen Going on Seventeen', from *The Sound of Music,* with Brendan O'Hea. Brendan couldn't resist sending me up as well, singing 'You are sixty, going on seventy', because he was always ribbing Siân and me about how old we were, and how amazing it was that we could get onstage at all.

I thought that was the end of my association with that musical, until the summer of 2010, when the BBC Proms decided to celebrate Stephen Sondheim's eightieth birthday by presenting an entire evening of his music and asked me to sing 'Send in the Clowns' once more. I have played some large theatres but nowhere as vast as the Albert Hall, and I have never been so scared in my life. The delay before I went on seemed endless. They kept saying, 'No, wait . . . wait . . . not yet . . . *Now* go on.' So that was why I was late coming down those steps onto the stage, to face that huge audience. Fortunately, I couldn't really see them at all, it just looked like a great sea of waving corn.

It was lovely to see Stephen again after all that time. Very sweetly he said afterwards, 'Come to supper with me at the Ivy.' 'What, now? I'm afraid I can't do that, I have to go home and look after my grandson.'

Singing at the Proms was another new experience I shall long treasure, and I did enjoy the knees-up finale with all the other singers, with Bryn Terfel on one side and Simon Russell Beale on the other.

The last play in the five-year cycle at the National was to be a new play by David Hare entitled *Amy's View,* but before I could get down to that I had a date with the film cameras which promised to be fun, but turned out to be very important too in changing my whole relationship with the world of cinema.

■ ■ ■ ■ ■

14
Mrs Brown and
'M'
1964–1996

■ ■ ■ ■

Before I appeared in *Mrs Brown* I had come to the firm conclusion that I had no real future in the world of film. This dated from my early days at the Old Vic, when I went for my first screen test. I walked in and they were perfectly nice to me, and then this man, having looked at me for a long time, said, 'Well Miss Dench, I have to tell you that you have every single thing wrong with your face.' So I just very quietly got up and left. I thought, There is no point in going on with this.

I had a tiny part in my first film in 1964, the thriller *The Third Secret,* and I only remember it for a most terrible faux pas I made. I met Vittorio de Sica, and when we were having a coffee together I asked him what he was doing next. He said, 'I am going back to Italy to make a little film.' I said, 'Will that be the first film you've made?' 'No, you remember a thing called *Bicycle*

Thieves?' Then it burst on me like a rocket in my head what I had said to this brilliant man.

The following year I was in *A Study in Terror,* in which John Neville played Sherlock Holmes and Donald Houston was Dr Watson. It was a hoary old piece really, and I gave rather a hoary old performance as Sally Young, who worked in a soup kitchen. Quite soon after that I was offered my first decent role, in *Four in the Morning,* directed by Anthony Simmons. I was a young mother with a crying baby, Norman Rodway was my husband, and Joe Melia was his drinking friend. The story was about a young girl whose body is found in the Thames, and we improvised our dialogue around the basic situation. We rehearsed in my flat in Regent's Park, and we filmed in Putney, which must be the noisiest location in the whole of London. It is on the flight-path to Heathrow, next to a railway bridge and a road bridge, and right opposite where the river barges came and dumped all their rubbish. So we never got any kind of a run on anything. Every time we were interrupted Joe Melia would sing that dreadful pop song 'Wagon Wheels'. You never do discover which girl is the corpse.

I only made one film in the Seventies, a

racing mystery by Dick Francis, *Dead Cert,* and that was really only because Michael was in it. Tony Richardson was the director, and he said, 'Why don't you come along and play Michael's wife? We'll have a lovely time.' We did too, but I found the final version a bit strange when I saw it.

I had some more small parts in films in the Eighties, including *Wetherby* by David Hare, *A Room with a View* with Maggie Smith for Merchant Ivory, and *84 Charing Cross Road* with Anthony Hopkins, directed by David Jones. None of these had mass box office appeal, and it was not until the mid-Nineties that I was suddenly offered a part in a series that most certainly did.

This was as the first female 'M' in the James Bond films, a change thought to be triggered by the recent real-life appointment of Stella Rimington as the first woman to head MI5. My predecessor as 'M' had been Bernard Lee, a very good actor whom I had worked with in my very first television play, directed by Peter Graham Scott. *GoldenEye* also had a new James Bond in Pierce Brosnan; it was lovely working with him, and it was a very good script. I don't think I realised at first what a huge responsibility I had in playing 'M', I was just really excited about it. Michael and Finty were mad about the idea too, Michael said, 'Oh, brilliant — Bond-woman!' The very first time that Pierce visited me at home, he stood in the doorway and said, 'Hi, boss,' and Finty did a very theatrical stagger back across the room.

Pierce and I got on very well indeed, and I loved the line I had rebuking him in one of our early scenes, calling him 'a sexist, misogynist dinosaur'. I became completely drunk with power, because I can't mend anything, or even put the ironing-board up properly. Suddenly here I am, typing in numbers and a huge screen comes up behind me, I have to look as if I have done it. I actually find it quite hard, because I am always talking about things that I don't understand at all well. But it is just so terribly glamorous playing 'M' in very glamorous surroundings, flying out to Nassau, staying at 'The One and Only', it seems so very chic somehow.

In the next Bond film, *Tomorrow Never Dies,* I even got to order Geoffrey Palmer about as Admiral Roebuck. I had to come down a flight of stairs and walk up to him to give him a dressing-down. Well, as he is much taller than me, I would have been giving him a dressing-up, so they said, 'Just a minute, go to your dressing rooms.' So we did, and when we were called back they had built what looked like a small hill. I walked down the stairs looking very fiercely at Geoffrey, then up this small hill so that I faced him on the same level — that was a good feeling.

I got on very well with Martin Campbell, who directed *GoldenEye,* but much less so with Roger Spottiswoode, the director of *Tomorrow Never Dies.* The car used to call for me at 5 a.m. to take me to the Frogmore Studios at St Albans, and I was often not getting home much before 10 p.m. Then a motorbike would deliver ten new pages of script for the next day, which I had to learn in the car. Later, at the editing stage, when I had to go in for the 'looping' (re-recording dialogue) things rather came to a head.

My regular driver Bryan took me in to London, and we got held up by a huge container van breaking down in Conduit Street, off Regent Street, so I rang in on Bryan's mobile phone and said, 'I'm so sorry, I'm right round the corner, but we've got caught because this huge lorry has broken down,' and they said that was fine. Bryan dropped me and said, 'It's just four doors down there.' So I jumped out and went down, and there was Roger standing at the door, calling, 'Come on, come on, come *on*.' I said, 'Did you not get my phone call?' He said, 'No,' and at that moment somebody came up and said, 'Yes, Judi, we did get your phone call.'

I simply couldn't shake hands with him. So I said, 'Did you see me the other day in Streatham?'

'Did I?'

'You know you did, I nearly ran you over.'

At that minute Barbara Broccoli came out of the back and said, 'Pity you didn't accelerate and do the job for all of us.'

Then we started to loop it, and he said to me in a very surprised tone of voice, 'You're very good at this.' That was really the last straw, and then I did say to him, 'You know, it was very off-putting indeed to have learnt the script, and at a quarter to ten the night before to get a loud knocking on the door by the courier with a new script. That's not fair.'

'Well, we didn't start with the right script in the first place.'

'That's hardly my fault.'

'Well, I apologise. By the way, would you like to be in my new film with Jonathan Pryce? My car's at your disposal to take you wherever you're going.'

'No, I'd rather walk.'

I can be really difficult when I want to be.

None of that was called for when we filmed *Mrs Brown*. It was originally shot for television, where John Madden had made his reputation as a director on many successful series. Douglas Rae of Ecosse Films offered it to BBC Scotland, with Billy Connolly named to play Queen Victoria's ghillie, John Brown. There had been much mischievous speculation down the years about just how close the relationship was between the Queen and her servant, and the original title for the film was taken from one of the contemporary cartoons — *Her Majesty Mrs Brown* — until John Madden changed it because he thought it gave away too much of the story. I was then sent the script by Douglas, and he came to see me at the National Theatre. He looked a little surprised when I got out my diary and asked, 'When do we start?' Then he said, 'I think you should know that Billy's first choice to play Queen Victoria was Bob Hoskins.'

I soon learnt more about Billy's sense of humour. Douglas arranged for Billy and me to meet for lunch on our own at Le Caprice, which seemed a rather incongruous choice for both of us really. I arrived a bit early, so I got out of the car and walked a bit, and when I went in they said, 'It's the table in the corner, and Mr Connolly's been and gone. He was sitting there just now.' He had gone to buy some cigars, and when he came back we started to talk, and then we started to laugh, and then he showed me — along with the rest of Le Caprice — the rings in his nipples.

We carried on laughing through most of the shoot, mostly, though not entirely, off-camera. John Brown is not a funny part, and I thought Billy was spectacularly good in it, and wonderfully professional. The biggest problem we both had was with my pony, Bluey, which kept breaking wind during the takes. There is a longshot near the beginning of the film, when I am on the pony and Billy is leading me, and Bluey farted at nearly every step. If you look closely you can see our shoulders heaving.

It was even worse up on the hill near Lochnagar, because it was windy, and ponies don't like the wind up their bums. It was impossible to set the scene, because the ponies were all moving around, and back to back, and then suddenly mine would walk away — it was terribly difficult to control. When I gave John Brown the sprig of heather, it was a miracle that we got within passing distance.

After that, in a scene where Billy had to lift me down off the pony, we eventually had to do twenty-one takes, because something of me would catch on something of him, or the pony moved or farted, or Billy's microphone caught on my costume . . . It went on for ages and ages. I should think the outtakes from that scene are pretty good. It may have been funny for us, but I kept hearing poor John Madden saying, 'We've got to do it again, because the light's going, we've got to get it in.' He was right, because it was one of those rare wonderful mornings with the sun coming through all the larches, it was absolutely beautiful.

For much of the rest of the time it was unbelievably wet when we filmed in Scotland, and very, very cold. The film was shot on a shoestring, and I only had two dresses. It was harder for the boys because they were all out on the hill, and when it rained all the kilts got absolutely sodden. When a kilt gets wet, the bottom becomes like a razor; that was what killed John Brown in the end, because his leg got infected. I remember at the end of a day's shooting exteriors we were all sitting round trying to get the circulation back into people's feet.

It was just as cold on the Isle of Wight in October, when we had to do the swimming scene. We all had rubber suits under our clothes, and you can't swim normally in a rubber suit; we all look like ducks in water because you don't sink. I had to come out of a little bathing machine, down some steps, and John Madden said, 'If I think it's OK for us to go ahead, I'll say go, and if not, don't get into the water.' But it was a glorious October morning, cold with bright, glittering sunshine, so it was OK. Also that morning I got all dressed in black with that kind of white hedgehog effect that Queen Victoria wore on her head, and when I was due on the set they said there would be a car to take me. I said I would just walk round there, since it wasn't far. As I walked down the path a bus full of tourists was coming along the drive to Osborne House, and they got a terrible fright because they thought they had seen a ghost.

Finty played one of my daughters in it, and John then cast other young girls who resembled her, so we looked like a real family. There were also good friends of mine: Richard Pasco as the Queen's doctor, and, once again, Geoffrey Palmer, as her Private Secretary. After she visits John Brown in his cottage alone, the two of them look askance at each other, as Geoffrey says, 'Don't even think it!' Their exchange of looks got such a laugh at the preview I told them both off: 'I think it's outrageous that the two of you get so many laughs without saying anything! Please, do you mind, it's my turn, I'm the Queen, you know.' Geoffrey had previously ticked me off during filming because I was word-perfect from the first day. 'Why can you do that for them, and not for Syd and me in *As Time Goes By*?'

At the end of a day's filming we would all meet up for dinner at the hotel, and then Billy would sit down with his pot of tea and start telling stories. We laughed so much that I would glance at my watch, wondering if I could get by on only five hours' sleep, and at the next glance on only four hours'. Despite all the problems with the weather, we had a wonderful time.

One night was not quite so wonderful. We were all having dinner in a pub, about nine of us, and a man began making a nuisance of himself. He was drunk, and he kept joining in and shouting at us. When one of the girls got up to go to the loo, he came and sat down. Billy said to him, 'Don't sit there, that's somebody's chair.' Then this man said, 'I've got a pub in Australia, can I take a photograph of the two of you?' Billy said very firmly, 'You can take *one* photograph,' just to get rid of him. The man went upstairs to bed, but then he came back down in his socks, and carried on shouting out. When I went up to bed, the proprietor said, 'Do you mind if I escort you to your room? I'm a bit nervous about that man.' About three days later, there in one of the Sunday papers was our picture, captioned, *Billy takes Judi to a secret hideaway.* Billy's language was unprintable.

We were still expecting *Mrs Brown* to go out on the BBC, but then the American producer Harvey Weinstein saw it and said, 'No, no, this is going to be a movie.' That meant that Billy and I had to go to America to promote it. As we left Heathrow, I picked up a newspaper and saw a big headline: 'Brown says the Queen must pay for her own helicopter.' So I cut it out and when I got to New York I had it made up into cards, which I sent to everyone. It was thirty-eight years since I had last visited with the Old Vic, and I fell in love with the country and the people all over again. When Finty rang my hotel and said, 'Can I speak to Dame Judi Dench?' the switchboard girl said, 'Is that all one word?'

Billy and I had to do so many interviews, one after another, that he couldn't take them seriously. When he was asked for the umpteenth time what it was like working together, he would scream, 'She's a nightmare, ooh nauseous, an absolute nightmare.'

Then they would ask me, 'Apart from *Mrs Brown* and "M", have you done anything else?' So I thought, Well, that is the whole of my theatre career gone swish, straight past my ear.

We had a wonderful week in New York and Los Angeles, and Larry Guittard came with me to the premieres in both places; we have stayed good friends ever since *A Little Night Music*. I thought that was it, never dreaming that I would be back again the next year, when to my great surprise I was nominated for an Academy Award for playing Queen Victoria. By then I was back at the National Theatre, playing in *Amy's View*.

■ ■ ■ ■

15
AMY'S VIEW AND
HOLLYWOOD
1997–1998

■ ■ ■ ■

I came to admire David Hare's gifts as a screenwriter when I worked on *Wetherby* and *Saigon — Year of the Cat,* especially after all the problems we had with the latter, so I was keen to appear in his new play *Amy's View* at the National Theatre when Richard Eyre asked me. My part was Esme, a successful actress who in the last act has lost all her savings in the Lloyd's Names insurance crash in the City. We had a particularly strong cast, including Joyce Redman, and Ronald Pickup and Samantha Bond, both of whom I had worked with before. But from quite early on I found David's script much more difficult than I expected. At the end of the first week I went for a costume fitting, and when I came back I went straight to Richard and said, 'You must let me go, I can't do it, I can't learn it.' I was in the most frightful state about it. I have never experienced anything quite like that before.

David's dialogue is very like that of Shaw or Wilde: you can go completely off-beam, it isn't naturalistic at all, it has its own metre, and you can hear it. It is because we don't speak correctly any more, so you suddenly think, Oh, the word comes there in the sentence, does it? David writes wonderfully rhythmically, and once you have learnt it, it is just a rhythm in your mind.

When I came home, Michael said to me, 'Pull yourself together, do what I do, go up and run a bath, get into the bath, and then you're not allowed to get out until you know three or four pages, or whatever you set yourself.' It was a wonderful way of learning, especially if you did it last thing at night. The difference between us was that Michael would come home and sit in the kitchen, and just work and work at learning lines, and I couldn't do that. He used to say to me, 'You learn the lines by osmosis.' That was true, I always had, but now I had to adopt Michael's version of learning Esme's lines. I would do an hour in the bath, just going at it every day. I hate working like that, but it was a necessity.

The other difficulty was having to smoke in the play. I don't like it at all. I started on the first day of rehearsal, but I dreaded it, I never developed a taste for it, and it made me very sick sometimes. But I could see that it was essential as punctuation in David's script. When my driver, Bryan, was waiting for me with the car one day, he overheard one woman say to another as they came out, 'She doesn't usually smoke in a play, does she?' as if it was me smoking and not the character in the play.

One journalist even said to me, when she interviewed me about *Mrs Brown,* 'Oh, I found it so irritating, you upstaging people looking for your cigarettes, I longed to shout out, "Sit down for goodness' sake and be quiet." ' That undermined me terribly. When we came to do it on the Friday night, and I got to the speech about the journalists, I absolutely let fly. Samantha Bond was playing my daughter, Amy, and she was so taken aback by this that she asked our wig lady, 'Has something upset Judi?' 'Why?' 'My God, she didn't half let fly about the journalists.'

After one performance, I was going on to dinner at the Ivy with Nigel Havers and his wife and parents. I had a bunch of visitors in my dressing room, so the others went on ahead, while Nigel waited to take me. When we got out of the car, we were surrounded by photographers, it so put me off that I didn't want to go any more. Another time I was waiting outside the Connaught for my old friend Pinkie Johnstone, now Kavanaugh, when I saw this man with a long-range lens, and wondered what he was photographing. Then my picture appeared in *OK* magazine, carrying a lot of Marks and Spencer bags, looking extremely cross, with a caption, 'Dame Judi knows how to shop.' He even followed us round to Scott's restaurant, and took more pictures of Pinkie and me sitting outside. I don't see how that is interesting, for one thing, and I really don't think that is anybody else's business.

David Hare was a huge comfort throughout the rehearsal period from the very beginning. A couple of weeks before we started he sent me a lovely note with a little appeal at the end:

Dear Judi,

Somebody sent me a tape of Mrs Brown. *I think it's one of your greatest performances. It's certainly your greatest film performance. I loathe the bloody monarchy, as you know, but even I found your grief for Albert and your relationship with the ghillie unbearably moving. It is great acting.*

I'm thrilled we start soon. No need to reply to this. Oh, one thing: why not be as good in my play as you are in the film?

Many congratulations.

> *Love,*
> *David*

He came to nearly every rehearsal, and it can sometimes be very off-putting to have the author there all the time, but he laughed at all the jokes every time, which was most encouraging. He said he was happy to do any rewrites if we were unhappy about anything, but asked us to say so earlier rather than later. I nearly asked him to change my entrance at the end of the play in a howling storm, when I had a bucket of water thrown over me before coming on. I said, 'That's going to make a *great* curtain-call, dripping wet!' but I could see what an effective moment that entrance was.

David was much less sympathetic to the audience at the fund-raising gala preview for the sponsors. I was more than a bit daunted myself on that occasion, but in fact that was quite a good thing. I was so frightened at the gala that it completely took the edge off the first night, which became a real work-in-progress night, whereas the gala had been utter white-hot fear.

I just thought to myself, Stuff you lot, I haven't worked forty years in the theatre to let a bunch of dinner-jacketed stiffs oppress me. I have got a job of work to do here, I have got to remember the lines. Part of the tension was caused by the large number of people in the audience who had lost lots of money in the Lloyd's Names crash, just like Esme in the play. At the supper afterwards one woman told me tearfully, 'That's my story too.'

David rather lost his temper with some of the sponsors when they criticised the play. Then he came shamefaced into my dressing room and said, 'Did you hear what I've done?' 'No.' 'I told them to get out. They said they were entitled to their opinion, and I said, "Yes but not to have free drink." ' That is such a funny argument, but David is like any of us — you are very raw and wounded at such a point.

Hal Prince came round afterwards one night, and said, 'You've got to come to New York with this.' I told him that I wanted to go to New York with it, but that Meryl Streep and Glenn Close had been to see it the week before, so I knew what was going to happen. The next morning Hal sent me a note, saying, 'Meryl and Glenn are too goddamn smart to try to muscle in on your role, come to New York.' We did eventually, but I had to go to America for a different reason long before we took the play.

We made another series of *As Time Goes By* during the run of *Amy's View,* and one day I was having lunch in the canteen at the BBC rehearsal rooms in Acton when Tor Belfrage (who took over as my agent when her husband Julian died in 1994) rang to say, 'You've been nominated for an Oscar for *Mrs Brown.*' That was the first I knew of it, and so that meant a lot of rushing about getting dresses, shoes and goodness knows what else. By then *Amy's View* had come out of the repertoire at the National, and transferred to the Aldwych for a continuous run. The nicest thing about that transfer was that Michael was going to do his one-man show, John Aubrey's *Brief Lives,* at the Duchess Theatre just round the corner, so we were able to travel home together.

The snag was that his opening night was the very night of the Oscars in Hollywood, and there was no way he could come with me, so I took Finty instead. My first re-action was that I couldn't go either, because I was in the theatre and I didn't approve of buying out performances to make such a thing happen. But Harvey Weinstein in-sisted, and Miramax bought out two nights of the play so that I could go to Los Angeles.

I thought that this was going to be such an extraordinary experience that I had better try to keep some sort of diary, so here are a few short extracts of some of the stranger happenings from 27 February onwards, when I first heard about my brief release from the Aldwych:

COUNTDOWN TO THE OSCARS!
or Will I be the only unlifted face in Hollywood?

Zandra Rhodes and Donatella Versace both offered dresses — but I shall go to Nicole Farhi and keep it in the family. (Mrs David Hare!!)

On Friday at the half a huge bouquet of blossom and yellow roses arrives at the theatre + a bottle of KRISTAL champagne from DUSTIN HOFFMAN, who had seen *Mrs Brown* and is v. complimentary. I shall be able to write a book entitled *My life with the stars!!*

3 March

Interview with Marylu Dent down the phone to LA. 'This may be indelicate but you seem to have a lot of energy for

someone of your age . . .' Veteran — old
— Old Guard, etc.

Tuesday, 10 March

8.00. Had to talk to James Nochty [I
couldn't spell Naughtie] for the *Today*
programme. Live!! I mumbled a lot and
didn't really come up with the goods.
    4.30. To Fouberts Place to meet Ni-
cole. She'd done several designs and we
chose one of them. We decided on the
grey organza not the frost.

Monday, 16 March

Fitting at 117B Fulham Rd with Nicole
and Barry & the design team. Saw a
wonderful trouser suit. They are altering
it for me. Got a 4-leaf clover from Van
Cleef & Arpels for luck. Turned down
Asprey!!!

19 March

Critics Circle Lunch. They all wished
me well. Fitting with Nicole 4.30. Tor
faxed me through diamond earrings
from VC & A's. Chose figure of eights

— they are <u>only</u> 50 thousand dollars a pair!

Saturday, 21 March

Long talk to P. Hall who rang to wish me luck. Note from Liam Neeson. Cards. Flowers from Pauline & John Alderton. GPS [Geoffrey Palmer] & Sal rang. After the show when I'd taken my wet dress off all the crew and company were waiting with champagne & a lovely card & Ronnie Pickup made a speech.

Sunday, 22 March

Got to Heathrow Terminal 4 and were met as we checked in. The staff at <u>Gatwick</u> had sent good wishes. Our dresses were <u>hand carried</u> to the plane — WE HOPE!! Phoned Mike. Called at last to the plane — <u>photographed.</u> Sat right at the very front of the plane L & R.

Champagne, lunch and crashed out for a while. Watched Morgan Freeman (what a good actor) on the TV. Invited on the flight deck for landing. At 10.30ish I went up on the flight deck and watched us coming into LA. Incredible. Met by v. nice man who escorted us through customs etc. Dress bag had been put with luggage. Tor met us & we all went to 4 Seasons. Then we bathed and changed and by 5.20 Tor, Gene Parseghian [William Morris Agency], Fints & I all went off in a S.T.R.E.T.C.H. limo along Rodeo Drive to the Beverley Wilshire Hotel. Finty got frightfully excited when she recognised it as the hotel used by Richard Gere and Julia Roberts in *Pretty Woman.* Up to a room to be interviewed by 4 or 5 reporters (all British). Then downstairs and into Harvey Weinstein's party [Miramax]. Saw Beverley, Veronica, Sinclair & Lisa [up for the Make-up Award for *Mrs Brown*]. Saw Dougal [Rae] & Jane, & Harvey who said H. B. Carter & I had to do a skit on *Good Will Hunting* [another of the Oscar-nominated films]. I nearly freaked out. Madonna & Demi Moore were sitting at the next table. Anyway — we did it and had to be 2 construction workers wearing hard hats. I was someone called CHUCKIE & had to say fuck a lot. It brought the house down.

Robin Williams was Mrs Brown but kept lapsing into Billy Connolly! We were given a box of chocs with a little

Oscar attached. When I opened it, it wasn't chocs, but a framed photo of John Madden talking to me as Queen Victoria.

After that I simply didn't have time to keep up the diary. The whole thing was absolutely wonderful, but it is like nothing we do here. You start getting ready at crack of dawn, there are hairdressers and people to do your nails, your feet, and goodness knows what arrives — permanent orange juice, and coffee, and strawberries dipped in chocolate.

After lunch I called Michael at the Duchess Theatre. He said they cheered a lot at the curtain call for *Brief Lives,* so then a great weight fell off us, and we were in the right mood to go to the Oscars. We got dressed and climbed into this vast limo. They said 'Are you ready for the red carpet?' but nobody prepares you for that. It is about a hundred yards long, with the bleachers going up so high, and absolutely packed full of people. It took me an hour to get along it, with all the cameras and interviewers. Finty said, 'Mama, look,' and up in the sky at that minute a plane had made a huge heart with a vapour trail, that was lovely. Then we went in, by which time my feet were killing me. As soon as I sat down I saw Vanessa Redgrave with Franco Nero, and we had a bit of a chat.

I remember just being hysterical with Finty and Helena Bonham Carter, saying, 'Just look at us, look at the dresses and jewels and things, and nothing to show for it.' There were five of us nominated — the other four were Helena, Julie Christie, Kate Winslet, and Helen Hunt who won it for her performance in *As Good as It Gets.* She was the only American nominee, and somebody said to us afterwards that of course none of the rest of us stood a chance because we had split the British vote four ways. When I went on to the Miramax party an interviewer thrust a microphone at me and said, 'A nation weeps.'

I said, 'Oh, *come on!*'

'You must be very disappointed.'

'No, I'm not disappointed at all. I didn't expect to win.'

I really didn't, and I wouldn't have missed the experience for anything. The whole event is amazingly tatty, and absurd, and we had a *wonderful* time. We flew back the next evening, landed at Heathrow on the Wednesday morning at 11.30 a.m., and I was at the Aldwych by 2 p.m. I had a couple of hours' sleep, and then went on. It was almost as if

I had never been away. The company kept telling me I had been robbed, but what really took me aback was the audience reaction that night. As soon as I made my first entrance they rose for a standing ovation, which never happens in London. I hugged Sam as Amy, and whispered, 'What do I do now?' She whispered back, 'Just go on hugging me.' To my astonishment the same thing happened every night that week.

A little later I did win the BAFTA Best Actress Award for *Mrs Brown,* and this time I could actually say I was robbed, as the statuette was stolen before I had even left the hotel. BAFTA were so quick in replacing it that I came to the conclusion this must happen all the time.

■ ■ ■ ■

16
SHAKESPEARE IN LOVE AND BROADWAY
1998–2000

■ ■ ■ ■

I so enjoyed working with John Madden on *Mrs Brown* that I wrote him a note after we finished filming, to say, 'I'll slouch in any doorway, or walk through the back of any shot for you in your next picture, that's a promise.' Some time later he rang me up and said, 'What I have in mind is not exactly any doorway or passing through the back of any shot.' So I said, 'Well, I'll do it, I shan't read it, I'll do it.'

The film was *Shakespeare in Love,* and the role was Queen Elizabeth I. She only had three short scenes, and I think that John must have been nervous that the part was not big enough, because when we next met at a BAFTA awards evening he said to me, 'Now we really need to sit down and talk.'

'You've changed your mind! You don't want me.'

'No, no, I just wanted to know that you liked the script, and still felt happy about doing the part.'

'Of course, I think it's wonderful.' But I couldn't resist taking advantage of his nervousness. 'It will be the same perf., you know, different frock.'

I shouldn't have joked about the frock, because that was the hardest part of the performance. It was tremendously heavy, it took two people to lift it on to me, and three people to do it up. I couldn't get out of it at lunchtime, and had to sit bolt upright to eat — it was agony. After the first fitting I rang up Sandy Powell, the costume designer, and said, 'Sandy, I don't think I should be at a great disadvantage with Gwyneth Paltrow. I think I should be able to look her in the eye.' He said that he thought the same thing, and then these vast platform shoes arrived, with six-inch heels, which were so uncomfortable to wear. They all called me 'Tudor Spice', and sometimes John Madden would say, 'Sorry, we'll have to go again, we caught a glimpse of Tudor Spice there.'

On top of that, there was the make-up, which took four hours to put on. Veronica Brebner did my make-up for both Queen Victoria and Elizabeth; she was up for an Oscar for each of them and never got it, which she should have done, because she was so meticulous. My hair had to be pinned, and then glued, the bald cap went on, and then it was all bled in. Then the make-up, then the wig, and then the head-dress. I wanted her to have bad teeth, and all her skin cracked, and they did get some terrible teeth made for me. But because it would be so huge on the screen, when your face is three times the size of your house, they said it would be too grotesque, and the Americans wouldn't accept that. So they just painted my own teeth brown, which looked bad enough.

Gwyneth was playing the invented character of Viola, the object of Shakespeare's love; the latter was played by Joseph Fiennes. Tom Stoppard had written the final version of the script, and we had a wonderful cast, including Colin Firth, Simon Callow, Tom Wilkinson, Antony Sher, Geoffrey Rush, Rupert Everett, Martin Clunes, Imelda Staunton, and Ben Affleck, so there was much press interest. Somebody made up a totally untrue story about Gwyneth and me, saying there was a frostiness between us, when we got on perfectly from day one, we never had a cross word. We didn't meet that much, because we didn't have many scenes together, but we had the most marvellous day sitting in the caravan, having a good laugh. When we took *Amy's View* to Broadway, she came to one of the earliest performances with her mother, the actress Blythe Danner, and brought her round afterwards. This malicious story about the filming really annoyed me; it seems as if when journalists don't have a story they will just make anything up, to try and cause trouble.

They even got wrong the story about the wonderful set that was created for the original Rose Theatre in the studio. It was so authentic that I begged them not to break it up after the filming finished. So they said, 'Well, you can have it if you like, we'll give it to you if you'll store it.' It was carefully dismantled at the end of shooting, and shipped off in sections to various storehouses in London and Manchester. Then the newspapers said I had bought it, which wasn't true, although I did find that the initial storage fees were quite high. There were various plans to rebuild it for use as a theatre, none of which have reached fruition yet, though I hope very much that it will return to life one day as a working playhouse.

Shakespeare in Love received thirteen Oscar nominations, including mine for Best Supporting Actress — much to my surprise. I was even more surprised when I actually won. I just thought, Well, I didn't get it for *Mrs Brown,* so I am certainly not going to get it for eight quick minutes with bad teeth. The lovely thing was that this time Michael was able to come with me, as well as Finty, because Miramax very generously invited both of them too. We went to their party the night before, and when we got there, who was first on in the cabaret? Me! I had to do Brenda Blethyn in *Little Voice,* so Finty quickly rehearsed me in a corner behind a pillar, and I had to wear a terrible red wig. The difficulty was that it was cocktail time, before you had even had a drink to get in the mood.

But the organisation of the awards ceremony was just as chaotic as before. We had to wait half an hour for the car downstairs, which seemed a very long time, and then we joined the convoy of stretch limousines. I vowed if I ever went again, I would go on the back of a motorbike. It was ridiculous, we were so late that they had locked the doors. They said, 'Oh my God, they wanted a shot of you when Whoopi Goldberg came in dressed as Elizabeth I.' They had to wait until a break and then smuggle us in.

Robin Williams was presenting the award, and when he looked down to read the name, Michael squeezed my arm and said, 'Jude, you've got it,' just before we heard him say, 'There is nothing like a Dame.' He said he could tell by the look on Robin's face. All I can remember after that is looking at Michael, standing up and kissing him, but I don't remember walking up all those steps. The only other thing I remember is Robin Williams curtseying; I don't remember the speech, nor anything about how I got off the stage.

I remember crying in a lift, completely overcome, and then meeting the immensely tall James Coburn, who had won Best Supporting Actor for *Affliction,* and having my picture taken with him, and then with Gwyneth, who won Best Actress. There were so many photographers, you are all blinded for a bit after all those flashlights going off. I had to go into lots and lots of rooms, where there were masses of people, and all the world's press asking, 'Why aren't you wearing diamonds?' I said, 'I'm not a diamond girl, I'm afraid.'

Then we went to two parties. The Governor's Ball was so beautifully done, in a wispy kind of sea-greeny-blue tent. But everybody only goes for twenty minutes, and then comes away again; nobody eats the food. There was a wonderful band, too, I thought it was terribly sad. In fact, I went up to a waiter and said, 'I'm so sorry about this.' I don't think they minded, but I minded, I thought it was terribly rude. We went on to the Miramax party, and I drank a lot of champagne.

The next day Michael and Finty went home, but I had to fly to New York, where *Amy's View* was due to open on Broadway. I was wandering about the airport at Los Angeles, and suddenly an air hostess came up to me and said, 'Would you like to get on the plane early?' So I said that would be very nice, and she said, 'Well, you might find it tricky otherwise.' That would never happen here. You could be in an awards ceremony the night before, and nothing would happen at all the next day. They put me in a first-class seat, right at the front of the plane. The only thing that we had not thought of was that every single person had to file past me as they came on board. So there was a lot of shaking hands and taking photographs, until I felt I had met the whole of the plane. I went to sleep on the flight, and when I woke up there were a lot of stick-on notes on the rug over me.

I was very tired when I arrived in New York, so I was glad to be met at the airport by my good friend James Triner, and driven to the apartment they had booked for me at the Sutton Building. It was overflowing with flowers and champagne, and the fridge was full of food, including caviar. That night I went with Larry Guittard to a cocktail party upstairs at Chez Josephine, run by the son of the cabaret star Josephine Baker. When we left to go out to dinner, everyone downstairs clapped. I thought this was so bizarre. Nobody knew me here before, now everyone seemed to know me. The Americans are so nice and welcoming, everybody stopped me on the street to say, 'Hi, Judi.' They are not intrusive, just absolutely open.

A lady who was serving in Bergdorf Goodman suddenly said, 'Oh my God! Look who's here!' and gave me the most enormous hug. Maggie Smith was also staying at the Sutton, and when we went into Tiffany's I said I might get her this very lurid bracelet. The young man was standing there looking down through the glass case, and started to say, 'Yes, good morning, ladies, can I help you . . . Ohh, my God,' as he looked up and saw us. Maggie and I were both in hysterics.

The American stage crew were a knockout. When we did Sunday matinees, everyone brought in something for brunch, and all of us, the actors and the crew, ate it together downstairs. Every other Saturday, between the two shows, the crew cooked a barbecue on the other side of the theatre, which was fenced in. That was so nice. We had a good company spirit at the National, but on Broadway we had it from day one. There was a proper feeling about telling the story, nobody competed with anybody. I still hear from the Barrymore crew.

David Hare had to change some of the dialogue for the American audience — 'spanner' to 'screwdriver', and 'Sainsbury's to 'supermarket'. They had no idea what a 'fête' was, very little knowledge of what the Lloyd's Names crash was all about, and the line 'I don't care if he's buggered the Dagenham Girl Pipers' went for absolutely nothing.

We had two weeks of previews before the first night, by which time all the critics had been. I said to Sam Bond, 'Honestly, we don't have to be worried about this, they've seen it, they've made up their minds.' We had the most glorious first night, with the kind of reception you only seem to get in America, which we then had on nearly every night during the run. I always got a round of applause when I came on, and most nights there were standing ovations at the end. Nobody normally stands up for you in England, that is not our fashion. Many things are different in the American theatre. The curtain never went up on time, it was always about ten past eight, it just isn't fashionable to go up on time. The cell-phones rang occasionally, despite the notices up in the foyer, but that now happens in England too — far too often.

The thing I never quite got used to were the wooden police barriers placed outside the theatre, to control the large numbers of autograph-hunters, which I had never experienced before. I had a wonderful driver called Mike to take me to and from the theatre, and sometimes after a show he had to wait for up to half an hour before I could get away. I would glance up at him leaning on the car, and he would say, 'They're selling them all.' The joke was that when Michael came over to see the show, I warned him in my dressing room, 'Wait till you see the crowds at the stage door, wait till you see,' and when we went out there was just one man standing there.

The trickiest audience came the night after the nominations were announced for the Tonys (the Antoinette Perry awards for performance in the New York theatre). We could feel the audience take several paces backwards, as if to say, OK, show me — which is exactly what happens at home too.

You can never predict that a play will be a success on Broadway just because it has been in London, or vice versa. Nobody ever quite knows how productions will cross the water. It is a very subtle thing, but you can never say whether or not something is going to be a success when it transfers. So I was rather pleased when one of the New York papers pronounced: 'This Dame is a class act.' To stop it going to my head, someone else asked, 'Is she a Dame as opposed to a broad?'

It was nearly forty years since I had been there with the Old Vic, so I went down to Greenwich Village and walked around with Larry Guittard, looking for my old haunts of that visit. When we walked past Julian's Bar, where we used to drink before, Larry said, 'Look at Julian's.' There were about fifteen men at the window, all waving; Julian's is a gay bar now. New York is just as beguiling today as it was on my first visit, the only difference between then and forty years earlier was that now I needed a rest every afternoon, whereas when I was there before I didn't. Then I hardly had any sleep at all, but I knew I couldn't do this show on no rest.

At the Barrymore Theatre I had the dressing room that Marlon Brando shared with

Karl Malden in *A Streetcar Named Desire.* I used to tell everybody that this was where Karl Malden used to go to the loo in the loo, and this is where Marlon Brando used to go to the loo in the basin.

One particular bonus for me was that the Barrymore was just down the road from the Brooks Atkinson where Tim Pigott-Smith was playing in *The Iceman Cometh.* So the black glove was going to and fro like all-get-out. It went wrapped around some flowers on Tim's first night, and came back to me the same way on mine. I had it given to him onstage the night that President Clinton went. At the beginning of Act II when I entered all dressed up carrying a bag and gloves, and had a line, 'Oh, let me take off this hat,' one night I nearly carried on the black glove with my own, until it was snatched out of my hand at the last minute. That glove whirled about quite a lot on Broadway.

Various parts of my life seemed to converge during that run. I was told that one night forty-two members of the *As Time Goes By* Internet Fan Club were coming to the play. So they were kept in the theatre after the performance, and I took them a tray of custard tarts from Mr and Mrs Lionel Hardcastle. When their chairman said,

'Shall I write to Mr Hardcastle?' I replied, 'That's not Mr Hardcastle, that's Geoffrey Palmer.' When I got back to the apartment there was a note awaiting me from Geoffrey, saying, 'I know that this is the night that I would be mobbed by the Internet crowd.' I think he would have been mobbed too, if he had been there. They were a very nice group. They had come from all over the country to see it, and most of them had not met each other before. *As Time Goes By* seems to be much better loved there than in England.

The American Shakespeare Guild has created the John Gielgud Award for Excellence in the Dramatic Arts, known for short by the award itself — the Golden Quill. This is given alternately for performances in America and Britain, and previous winners have included Derek Jacobi, Kevin Kline, Ian McKellen, and Zoe Caldwell, so I was thrilled when they gave it to me during the run on Broadway. Several people in the company took part in the event.

David Hare reminded me of a letter that I had quite forgotten, when he had written to me before we ever met about one of my early performances. He read out my reply with great relish: 'You call me beautiful, you call me brilliant, I notice you don't call me tall.' Christopher Plummer recalled our times together with the RSC in the Sixties, and Keith Baxter read out a sweet note from John Gielgud himself, whose name made this award so very special. The previous winner, Zoe Caldwell, presented me with the hugely heavy Quill, and said to the film people in the audience, 'You can *lease* her now and then, but just remember: she *belongs* to the theatre.' I could hardly think of what to say after all this, but I was anxious to pay tribute to Sir John himself, and how he had restored my confidence all those years ago in *The Cherry Orchard.* (The following year, when the Shakespeare Guild gave the award to Kenneth Branagh, I stepped into Zoe's shoes and presented him with the Quill in the Middle Temple in London.)

Because *Amy's View* was such a success, the Barrymore management wanted to extend the run, but I refused, saying I had to get home to be a wife and a mother again. Oddly enough, I have not been offered any more theatre work in America, only films, a couple of which I accepted.

■ ■ ■ ■ ■

17
ITALY ON STAGE
AND SCREEN
1998–1999

■ ■ ■ ■ ■

The previous chapter made my life seem more planned than it ever really is, but for clarity it seemed best to follow on the filming of *Shakespeare in Love* with the subsequent Oscars ceremony and my time on Broadway. In reality there was a gap of something like a year between finishing the film and going to America, during which I did another play and a couple of films.

The play was *Filumena* by the Italian Eduardo de Filippo, directed by Peter Hall. My co-star once again was Michael Pennington, who had been agitating for ages for us to do it together. I hadn't seen Joan Plowright in the part in 1977, but I knew that she had been a great success. Filumena is a former Neapolitan whore who has borne three sons and never told her lover Domenico which one is his. She tricks him into marriage at last by pretending to be on her deathbed, a trick he has just discovered

297

as the play opens. So Michael had to storm on to the stage in a towering fury, shouting at me for deceiving him. We used to wind up for that opening by shouting and chasing each other up and down in the wings before we went on.

I can't think of another play that opens with an outburst of such intensity, and it took me a while to get used to it. At first I thought the play was very slight, but after I had done it for a while I realised that it wasn't slight at all. John Gunter had designed a brilliant set, which I didn't really understand until halfway through. Then I thought that of course this was an Italian story, and here was a table in an Italian house which everybody sits round but is never used, everyone walks past it. The more we did it, the more I reckoned the play, and we had a hugely good time doing it.

But the first night was nearly a disaster. I completely dried on my line: 'I don't suppose you know those hovels in San Giuvanniello, in Virgene, in Furcella, Tribunale, Palunetto . . .' I can hardly believe that I can still rattle them off now, but that night I couldn't remember a single Italian place-name. So instead I said every kind of pasta I could think of, fusilli and vermicelli, and valpolicella — a lot of Italian food and wine, because I had been having it for three months filming in Italy.

Also on the first night I jumped from Act I to Act III, I skipped a whole amount of plot; that gave me such a fright. Michael steadied me, he cleverly and imperceptibly moved me from Act III back to Act I again. He is so cool-headed inside, even if I did see the whites of his eyes when I did it. But I really thought I had blown it on the first night. I was terribly depressed afterwards. We fully expected the worst from the reviews, but they were very enthusiastic, so we must have got away with our improvisations. The box office was besieged, and they had to schedule some extra matinee performances to meet the demand. By then, we didn't mind that, we were so enjoying it. I remember saying to Michael one night, 'I've never been so happy on stage,' and he said, 'Well, neither have I, oddly enough.'

Whereas I could not, in all honesty, say quite the same for my previous filming experience in Italy, just before *Filumena*. *Tea with Mussolini* should have been just as wonderful. Franco Zeffirelli was directing, and the others in the cast included Maggie Smith, Joan Plowright, Paula Jacobs, Lily Tomlin and Cher. We were playing an assorted group of expatriates living in Italy just before Mussolini entered the war, and my Michael played the English Consul who tries to persuade us all to leave before we were interned. The locations were in Florence, San Gimignano and Rome, which could hardly have been nicer, and Franco seemed to have as much boundless energy as I remembered from *Romeo and Juliet* forty years earlier. He was charming, entertaining and funny, and part of the story was based on his own early life. I wouldn't have missed it for the world, working with Maggie again after such a long time, and also making a friend of Joan, whom I had not really known properly before.

When Franco was directing, he had this wonderful old dog that was carried behind him in a box. We were going to do a scene in a garage one morning in Rome, and there were Maggie, Joan, Lily, Paula and myself, all made up with our wigs and costumes, and then suddenly Franco changed his mind about the scene. He said he didn't want to do it then, he would do another scene. He said to Joan and Maggie and me, 'Why don't you go to the villa and swim?'

So we went to his villa, and we were all swimming very carefully, with nobody daring to get wet hair. Then we heard a lot of barking, and Franco had come back for lunch with three of the actors playing carabinieri, so we all had to race out and dry ourselves, and rush back to the dingy garage. It was far from the best-managed film schedule I have experienced, and the crew kept changing.

I was this rather scatty bohemian art-lover, and some of my scenes in the script never got filmed at all. Some of those that were shot never made it into the final film, but that is the nature of the film business; they can't do that to you in the theatre. There was one line from Cher that I doubted would ever hit the screen. She was supposed to say, 'Do I know Hester? I wouldn't trust her as far as I could throw her.' She obviously thought that was a bit weak, so she said instead, 'Do I know Hester? I wouldn't trust her as far as I could throw Musso's fat ass across the room.' Unsurprisingly that got cut too.

We even had disputes about the hotels booked for us, until Joan Plowright put her foot down. When we got to Rome we went to the hotel, and were sent up in a lift with a porter. He just said to me, 'That's your landing,' so I said, 'Oh, thank you very much,' and got out to find my room. It was a very dark room, and the air-conditioning didn't work. It was appalling, but I hadn't been in it for five minutes before the phone rang, and it was Joan. 'Darling, we're leaving here, it's a knocking-shop, I've heard two at it on my way up.' So we walked around Rome looking for a hotel. We went to the Majestic, and she insisted on seeing the rooms. She was so wonderful; she said, 'Lady Olivier would like a suite of rooms, we want at least three, because Maggie won't want to go to that knocking-shop.'

In the end we went to the Eden Hotel, and she said, 'Have you got three nice suites here? We only had rooms at the other hotel.' They said they did, so she said, 'We'll have them. Dame Maggie Smith, Dame Judi Dench, and Lady Olivier, we'll have the lot.' But they were not available until the next day, so we had to go back for just one night, which was awful. The dining room was underground, and it was all self-service.

Maggie had gone home for the weekend, so she had a terrible time when she got back, trying to find us. First she went to the original hotel, where they told her we had checked out, and as Joan had booked us in at several hotels before we found the Eden, poor Maggie had done the scenic journey round Rome before she finally found us at the Eden.

The three of us spent a lot of time on their lovely roof terrace. To begin with, they told us that we couldn't eat out on the terrace, we could only eat in the restaurant. But after a while, I think they were so ashamed of us that they said we could eat round the corner, they hid us from the public. So we ate there every evening when we came in. The film company said they wouldn't pay for the Eden, we would have to pay the extra ourselves. But since we were doing publicity interviews at the Eden for the film, Joan and Maggie both said, 'We're sorry, but if we're being interviewed there, we're not paying for it, and we're not going to be interviewed any more unless you pay for it.' So in the end they did.

I remember Maggie and I having the most extraordinary experience when we went to see the Pantheon. It was brilliant sunshine outside, and when we came in out of the sunshine the whole place was very misty. Round the dome two white gulls were circling, they didn't even flap their wings, they were just cooling off in there for about ten minutes, and we couldn't take our eyes off them.

Next I had my third stint as 'M' in *The World Is Not Enough,* directed by Michael Apted this time, who I thought was brilliant, and it was a very good script. I had complained that I never got taken to any of the exotic locations in the film, so this time they said they were going to take me to Scotland, and to Turkey. The nearest I got to either was a painted background of Loch Lomond, and a Winnebago trailer with Innsbruck stuck on it, so I could say I had been in Innsbruck. It is only recently that I have been taken to locations in Prague and Nassau.

What I enjoyed most was the day at Swindon when 'M' had to go up in a little glass helicopter, which looked like a see-through insect. It was a very blustery day, and up we went, with my assistant Colin Salmon in the back, and a whole lot of bodyguards for 'M'. We had to wait for the action and then come swooping down; we did that three times to get the shot, and it was thrilling, I loved it. That took the whole day, and when I got home I happened to look at the call sheet. On the list was 'M's stunt-double'. So I guessed that they must have thought I was going to say, No, I won't go up in a helicopter. I was really pleased that it hadn't come to the crunch.

Sophie Marceau was brilliant in the film, and in the scene I was doing with her I was riveted by the coat she was wearing, and thought I must draw it, so that perhaps I could get it copied. I asked our costume designer, Lindy Hemming, where it had come from, and she said, 'Oh, they're in Beauchamp Place, do you want to see if they've got a coat like that?' and I said, 'Yes, please.'

My agent, Tor, came to see me at lunchtime and asked me, 'Who do you want to do your clothes for the Oscars?'

'I don't know, Sophie Marceau's clothes in this are absolutely beautiful.'

'Well, I'll go to them and ask if they would like to supply some stuff, or would they like to see you about fitting something.'

About ten minutes after Tor had left, Lindy came in to say, 'Those people are very keen that they should do some clothes for the Oscars.' So I had already asked her, and they had already offered, and we hadn't known. By sheer serendipity, the Bond film provided the clothes I needed for going to the Oscars with *Shakespeare in Love.*

If 1999 was a watershed year for me, it was not because of the Oscar and my time on Broadway, but because of something far more important in my family life. That was when we first learned of Michael's illness, and I came home to nurse him.

■ ■ ■ ■

18
MICHAEL
1999–2001

■ ■ ■ ■

Towards the end of the run of *Amy's View* in New York Michael became ill, so when I came home I didn't work at all from July to October 1999. Then I continued to turn down all the theatre work I was offered in favour of a few short spells of filming, so that I could be at home with him most of the time.

The first of these was *The Last of the Blonde Bombshells,* for BBC Television, and it had the most brilliant and funny script by Alan Plater. I played the youngest member of a wartime girls' band, who decide to get back together years later for one last concert. The others were Leslie Caron, Olympia Dukakis, Cleo Laine, Joan Sims, Billie Whitelaw, June Whitfield, and Ian Holm who was dodging the Army so was forced to play in drag. None of us were musicians, of course, so we had to have lessons in how to finger our instruments convincingly, even though the actual music would be dubbed in later. I had to play the saxophone, and my teacher was Kathy Stobart, a member of Humphrey Lyttelton's Band.

Kathy was marvellous. I learned how to play a scale on the saxophone, even though I found it very hard to make it look authentic. The family were all hugely relieved when I had finished the film, and stopped practising on the saxophone at home. Everyone used to go out of the house when I did it, including the cats, who just took off, they absolutely hated it.

I had to play the tenor sax, and Billie Whitelaw was on the alto sax, and there was one scene with all of us on the school stage with our instruments beside us. Somebody said, 'Now we'll play for you,' and we had to pick them up and play. But Billie had picked up the one on her left instead of her right, so she was playing mine, and I had no instrument to play. We laughed so much about that, but it was easy to tell that we weren't really professional musicians. Alan Plater later adapted his screenplay for a stage musical, but then of course they had to find people who could actually play the instruments as well as act. I have met people who saw it and had a lovely evening, so it must have come together very well.

I played a much less happy-go-lucky character in my next film, *Chocolat,* as a very grim-faced grandmother, who is charmed by the arrival in a French village of a young chocolate maker, played by Juliet Binoche. All my scenes were shot here, because I couldn't go away to France, and the reconstruction was wonderful, but in my big birthday party scene we had the most torrential rain you could imagine. There was a great big blue canopy over us outside, and we kept shooting bits of the scene whenever there was a lull in the rain. The crew had to come with big poles every few minutes and push at the canvas, to shake off the great pools of water which had accumulated. I kept thinking this was ridiculous, we were meant to be in this idyllic wonderfully sunny place in France. However, I did get to dance with Johnny Depp, and when it was cut out of the film I was very miffed.

I couldn't be mad with the director for very long. Lasse Hallström was Sweden's equivalent of John Madden. I had exactly the same feeling of somebody in total control on the set, yet very laid-back with time for a joke, and time to talk to you. I trusted Lasse in the same way that I trusted John, or Trevor Nunn, or Richard Eyre, or

Peter Hall, or Anthony Page. So I was thrilled when he asked me to be in his next film, *The Shipping News,* to be shot in Nova Scotia and Newfoundland. But that had to be put on hold until the following year.

Michael had got progressively weaker. The original diagnosis of pleurisy had been wrong, and it was discovered that he had lung cancer, which was now inoperable. He tried to carry on working for a while, mostly in radio, recording more of the Conan Doyle mysteries, playing Dr Watson to Clive Merrison's Sherlock Holmes, but then he had to give that up.

One thing that especially pleased us both was his appointment in November 2000 to the Order of St Gregory, the Papal equivalent of a knighthood. He wanted to receive it in Westminster Cathedral, but he could no longer face the journey to London, so it was conferred at home in Surrey, on 10 January 2001. Afterwards Michael said to me, 'I wish we could have a rerun of today.' I said, 'I wish we could too.' It was a huge honour, and very rare, so it was terrific that that happened.

Michael died the next day, and Finty and some close friends took the burden off me of telling everybody. Our churchgoing had always been very ecumenical: Michael went to Mass and I went to my Quaker Meeting, but we often attended our local Anglican church together, so that was where we held the funeral, with four priests sharing the prayers. To begin with, we had thought of only having a small family funeral, but so many friends rang up and said that they wanted to come, that in the end the church was packed to overflowing, with standing-room only at the back. The readings were by Clive Merrison, Richard Henders, and Roger Rees, who flew in specially that morning from New York.

If a funeral is to be a wonderful farewell, that is what it was, and I believe it was exactly what Michael would have wanted. Trevor Nunn delivered the most beautiful and touching address, part of which I would like to quote here:

I think it's only possible to discern the capacity for great acting in performers who themselves have a greatness of spirit, who have insight and burning moral passion that is transfiguring. I am talking of Mike's soul, his largesse and generosity of spirit, so evident in his encouragement of young and emergent talents; his spirit, which made him and Judi wonderful partners through all the hills and valleys of life, whose shared bravery and optimism in the last two years have been a beacon to all of their friends, as we have marvelled at their strength.

I remember them courting, as if it was last year, in Stratford, and London, and Australia — and when they got married, Mike said to me he was in the grip of feelings beyond any happiness he had ever dreamed of. He told me more than once that his favourite line in Shakespeare was 'Lady, you have bereft me of all words' — because, when he was with Jude, he knew exactly the full extent of what Shakespeare was saying. A fine romance indeed.

I was so moved by this that I asked Trevor to give it again at Michael's Memorial Service six months later at the Actors' Church in Covent Garden. We held it on 9 July, Michael's birthday, and the speakers this time included John Moffatt, Kenneth Branagh and Ned Sherrin. Patrick Doyle sang two of his songs for Ken's film of *Henry V,* in which both Michael and I had appeared.

I had spent several months nursing Michael at home after my brief stint in *Choco-*

lat, which was my longest time off work since giving birth to Finty, and it was Michael who had urged me to go back to work after she was born. After he died, I felt that he was again influencing me to pick up the strands of my career. During that long break my agent had refused to commit to any offers, and there were only three films that I was at all keen to do — *The Shipping News, The Importance of Being Earnest,* and *Iris.*

Tor had kept them all on hold, but about a month after Michael died she rang me to say that by some miracle of scheduling it looked as if I could just manage to do all three, though the timing would be very tight. There was only a day between finishing one and starting the next, and at one point I was alternating between the shooting of two of them. The fact that the powerful American film producer Harvey Weinstein was involved in the production of all of them obviously helped to synchronise the schedules.

Some people may have thought that I was running away from the fact of Michael dying, but then I had a lot of letters telling me, 'Do work, it's the best thing,' from people who had shared my experience. It certainly left me no time to dwell on things. There were two separate periods of filming in Canada, and in the five-week gap I filmed *Iris*. As soon as we had finished the second lot of filming on *The Shipping News* I flew back and went straight to West Wycombe, to start shooting on *The Importance of Being Earnest*. I naturally began this marathon in a rather fragile state, and when Lasse said to me on arrival, 'I can't imagine what you must be going through, it must be ghastly for you,' I completely went to pieces. But then I pulled myself together, and I was fine after that.

The first thing I did in Nova Scotia was to work with a voice coach, because the Newfoundland accent was very, very difficult. The good thing was that some of the crew were from Newfoundland, and they told me whenever I got anything wrong. So I was not best pleased when one film critic said that my accent was simply appalling. I long to meet Andrew O'Hagan to ask him how long he was in Newfoundland, and how well he knows it, because I was actually pulled up on every word if it was not right.

Kevin Spacey was cast as my nephew, and we had met during my time on Broadway when he was playing the lead in *The Iceman Cometh*. I had got him to deliver the black glove to Tim Pigott-Smith onstage with President Clinton in the audience, so he already knew all about that game. Tim airmailed the glove to Kevin, and got him to return the compliment on camera. He chose the moment of maximum embarrassment. Agnis Hamm hated her late brother, so she dumped his ashes in an outhouse and peed on them. Naturally this shot was being delicately filmed, until Kevin reached in from below with the glove on a long stick and tickled my bottom with it. I leapt into the air screaming, and it was some while before we could complete the scene.

Kevin was terrific in the film. He is a big joker and a brilliant mimic, he has a good ear for other actors' voices. When we were on the Parkinson show together later, he did a wicked impersonation of Ian Mc-Kellen. He made me laugh incredibly from the very first day. He is a remarkable actor, and we just had a marvellously funny time. There was a running joke in Newfoundland that everybody but me kept seeing the whales offshore, and I was dying to see them. Kevin and I were in the middle of shooting a scene facing each other, and there was a low window behind me. I had to say my line and then turn and walk away. Just at that moment I heard somebody shout, 'A whale,' and I ducked down to peer out of the window. He never let me forget that impulse — in the middle of a scene! Well, it wasn't quite right, was it?

During the second period of shooting we had a three-day break one weekend when we were at Port Rex, and Kevin said, 'Why don't you come to New York?' I had to have a photograph taken for a magazine, and they were coming up to the location, so I rang them in New York and suggested I went to them instead. All the crew who were going home went to St John's airport, where it had been foggy for three days. When the fog lifted, which it finally did that morning, there were four hundred moose all over the airfield. They fired shots in the air, they tried everything, but nothing would move the moose, so none of the crew got away, they spent the entire weekend at St John's.

Luckily, we had gone to Gander Airport, where the five of us flew to New York: Lasse, Julianne Moore, Kevin, his make-up artist Tania, and myself. We had the most incredibly enjoyable weekend, we saw *The Producers* and *Proof* on Broadway, and I learnt to ride a motor-scooter. Kevin was staying at the Trump Tower, and my hotel, the St Regis, was just round the corner. I went to see him one morning and he said, 'Right, we've got to have a rehearsal.' So we had a rehearsal on this Zappy power-assisted scooter, and I drove straight down a corridor into a lady carrying a great pile of sheets and towels. Kevin said, 'This is no good, we'll take it down to the park.' So off we went to Central Park. I suddenly got the hang of it and raced off to Central Park West; it was absolutely thrilling. Luckily there were no paparazzi around in the park, or I shudder to think what the headline would have been. Then we had to go back to start work again, but it was a wonderful break.

Since he took over as Director of the Old Vic, Kevin has tried several times to get me to join his company, and I would have loved to, but we haven't been able to get the dates to work yet. I still want to go back there, I think it is just admirable the way he has stuck at it, even though he has been given a really rough time by the London critics. It is our gain that he is running the Vic, and I hope everybody realises it soon, because he really loves that theatre, he cares for it, and wants to make it a real success.

I was grateful that they split my filming schedule on *The Shipping News* to allow me to play Iris Murdoch in between, but it was occasionally difficult to concentrate totally on the character I was playing. I emailed Kevin when I came back the first time, and wailed, 'I don't know whether I am Agnis Murdoch or Iris Hamm, I don't know *who* I am!'

Fortunately I had Richard Eyre and Jim Broadbent to keep me on the right track. Both their mothers had died of Alzheimer's, so I was always able to check with them on how they behaved in those last months. Iris Murdoch was my heroine anyway, because I had read all her books, and I watched television interviews with her. Kate Winslet was playing the young Iris, and she watched the same interviews, which was terribly helpful to both of us. But it was hard to make, because of the number of people who knew her and were friends of hers, and she had died so comparatively recently. It had been a bit easier with Queen Victoria, and even easier with Elizabeth I.

One of the most demanding scenes comes near the end of the film, and was shot on the beach at Southwold. Iris was by then far gone into the mists of Alzheimer's, and she dances with her old university friend Janet, played by Penelope Wilton, to the music on the radio. It was supposed to be in the summer, but we were filming it in October, and I was the coldest I have ever been, colder even than Newfoundland. We were wearing thermal underwear under our dresses to stop ourselves visibly shivering on camera.

One day in Oxford, moving from one location to another, I couldn't resist going and looking at the house where Iris had lived with John Bayley. I knew that John was away, but there was a window open, and his car was unlocked outside, and that told me so much about how they had lived together. I thought that Jim Broadbent was just phenomenal as John Bayley, and when I saw the two of them at the film premiere, apart from Jim looking about three feet taller, it was just uncanny seeing them together.

Hugh Bonneville played the young John Bayley. He and Jim studied each other in the role, and the similarities in their mannerisms were so marked that a lot of people in America, who didn't know either actor, thought that Jim played the part all the way through, which is a tribute to both of them. Jim won the Oscar for it, and quite right too, it was very exciting to be there with him that night.

We found that we had several things in common: we had both gone to Quaker schools, and we have very much the same sense of humour. In the first week I asked him, 'Do you have a cat?'

'Yes, I have a cat, he's called Naughty.'

'What a great name for a cat.'

'Not so hot when you're sitting in the vet's waiting room with a whole lot of other people, and they come out and call "Naughty Broadbent".'

Jim was one of the speakers when I was given the BAFTA Fellowship, and he warned me beforehand that he felt he had to take the jokey line, so I said, 'Please do.' With a wonderfully deadpan face he launched into a surreal description of how he discovered 'the real Judi, the one the public don't see, and it was a revelation. Who of you knew, for instance, that she is over six foot tall and massively built? How many of you are aware that her strong Birmingham-Russian accent, which she so valiantly struggles to overcome in her stage and screen work, is in real life almost impenetrable? And it is a mark of her extreme professionalism that it was the very last week of filming before I even realised that she had a prosthetic limb.' The audience found this just as funny as I did, and I was very glad that both he and Billy Connolly seized the opportunity to send me up.

No sooner had we wrapped on the last day's filming of *The Shipping News* than I was on the plane home to report for duty at West Wycombe in my second portrayal of Lady Bracknell, this time on film.

■ ■ ■ ■

19
LADY BRACKNELL
AND SOME OTHER
GRANDES DAMES
2001–2006

■ ■ ■ ■

The day after I got back from Newfoundland I was in a very different costume for Lady Bracknell, on location at West Wycombe. It was nearly twenty years since I had played her on stage for Peter Hall, now Oliver Parker was directing the film. The only other member of that 1982 National Theatre company to join me in the cast of the film was Anna Massey as Miss Prism. Oliver cast Finty as my younger self in a flashback, and he gave his father a walk-on part for the scene at the railway station when I arrived. As a student at Oxford, Peter Parker had been a famous King Lear in an OUDS production, and much later as Sir Peter he was in charge of British Rail. So I couldn't resist ad-libbing a line as he opened the door of my carriage: 'To whom do I complain about the delays?' But Oliver obviously thought that this was far too much of an in-joke, and cut it out of the film.

The costumes were very striking. My hats were so high that I couldn't get into an ordinary car to take me up from the car park to the house, and I had to travel in a golf buggy. I was wearing what looked like two foxes having a fight over my shoulders, so it was rather appropriate that our presence was noted in the local parish magazine in the Nature Notes:

Spotted in June at West Wycombe:
Long-eared owl, A4010 side of West
    Wycombe Hill
Dame Judi Dench in costume, main gate
    of Park
Stoat chasing rabbit in the cricket
    meadow

I loved the billing — after the long-eared owl, but before the stoat. It was sent to me by one of Geoffrey Palmer's friends, Ivor Herbert, who knew that it would appeal to me.

Lady Bracknell seemed to herald a run of formidable ladies of a certain age. Peter Hall asked me to play a grande dame of the American theatre — Fanny Cavendish, in *The Royal Family.* This was the 1927 Broadway comedy based on the Barrymore acting family, and written by George S. Kaufman and Edna Ferber. He had just formed his new Peter Hall Company, and this was to be its first production, in one of my very favourite theatres, the Theatre Royal in the Haymarket, with a cast including Peter Bowles, Julia McKenzie, Toby Stephens, Philip Voss and Harriet Walter. Harriet was playing my daughter, Julie Cavendish, and we had a scene where she talked of giving up acting to marry the man she loved. To Fanny this seems unimaginable, and she insists that Julie will regret it.

Toby Stephens, the son of my longtime friend Maggie Smith, was playing my son Tony, a Hollywood star just like John Barrymore. He was always fencing up and down the grand sweeping staircase on the set, and had great fun striking dramatic poses as if he were Barrymore in front of the film cameras. After the run of the play I was due to make my next Bond film, and Toby told me that he was doing a screen test for the villain. The producers said they would let him know, but kept him waiting for several weeks for a decision. He thought that the long delay meant that he wasn't going to be chosen, but as we were all making up one night suddenly we heard this tremendous shout from the top of the theatre. Toby charged down the stairs, and when we all came out of our dressing rooms he said, 'I've got the part!' We were all thrilled for him, and the play had an extra buzz that night. When he reached his line, 'Oh God, I hate pictures,' we all involuntarily went 'What!?' quite unrehearsed.

The press reactions to the production were mixed, and it was playing at an extraordinary time. On 11 September 2001 the world had been shaken by the devastating attacks on the Twin Towers in New York, and our play opened in November. The number of air travellers dropped dramatically, especially from America, whose theatre-loving tourists are so important to the West End (but the loyal members of the *As Time Goes By* Internet Fan Club were not so easily deterred). Several plays were forced to close much earlier than expected, but the home audiences flocked to see *The Royal Family,* which was sold out for most of the run.

My few weeks filming as 'M' again in *Die Another Day* sadly did not include any scenes with Toby Stephens; I was stuck in the studio, and he was doing all the glamorous things like parachuting into Buckingham Palace. Then I found myself back at the Haymarket in a new play by David Hare, *The Breath of Life.* This was a two-hander with Maggie Smith, and we hadn't appeared onstage together since our Old Vic days. There was in effect a third character, Martin, now dead, whose life we had both shared as wife or mistress, which set up the tension between the two women. The play was only ninety minutes long, but it was very intense and wearing to play, so much so that I declined the invitation to take it to Broadway, which rather upset both Maggie and David.

Instead I went back to Stratford for the first time in over twenty years to play the Countess in *All's Well That Ends Well.* We did it in the Swan Theatre, which had been a rehearsal room in my previous time there. It was a play I didn't know, I had never worked with the director Greg Doran, and it was good to be part of the RSC again — I am still so fond of that company. There are not many parts in Shakespeare that I can play now, and the Countess was a rewarding part in a play that is not seen very often. I loved it, and I loved being back at Stratford, because I have many friends there, and I know the area so well. Finty was very keen for me to go back, as she had grown up there and also loved it.

Later we brought *All's Well* into London at the Gielgud Theatre, where I succumbed to my weakness for walking-on in other people's productions. The RSC production of *Les Misérables* was playing at the Queen's Theatre, just at the other end of the block from the Gielgud. The Countess is off for a long while in the middle of the play, and I thought it would be thrilling to be able to put in my CV that I had been in *Les Mis.* I got them to make me a costume for it, got out of the Countess's costume, and raced along to the wings of the Queen's. The cast knew I was coming, but I didn't know any of them. Someone said, 'All you do is, you go in and put that stool down there. Then you will hear a shot in the middle of the barricades, and that's you being shot. Then we'll help you off.'

So I said, 'Fine, absolutely fine.' I got ready for it, then I suddenly thought that this was the actor's nightmare. It is like saying, 'What is the play, what is the part?' I thought, What am I doing? I went on, put the stool down, we were all singing, then came the shot, I went, 'Aaaargh!' and collapsed on to the floor. These two actors came up to me to help me off, and said, 'You've only been shot in the arm.' I thought that this guest appearance would be our little secret within the RSC family, but a couple of days later the story appeared in the *Evening Standard,* and I have never been allowed to forget it.

While we were doing *The Breath of Life,* Charles Dance came to see Maggie and me to ask if we would like to do *Ladies in Lavender,* which was to be his first film as a director. We said yes straight away, but then he had great difficulty in raising the money to make it, which dragged on for months, with none of us knowing if it would ever happen. We agreed to defer being paid, and everyone took a cut in salary, including Charles, to get it started. Then suddenly in the middle of filming the backers threatened him with the fact that they had run out of money, and nobody in the crew would come back the next day.

This must have been a great strain for Charles, but he never let it show; he was a completely natural director. We knew he was a good actor, of course, but he acted the part of the director absolutely convincingly, because you couldn't see the joins. He was remarkably assured, he knew exactly how he wanted something to be shot, and how he thought it should be. We had a glorious October, filming it on location in Cornwall, in Prussia Cove. It was so warm that at lunchtime the crew just dived into the sea for a swim. Maggie and I couldn't join them, because we were all wigged and made up, so we just played furious amounts of cards in the top attic of this little house.

This time we were playing sisters who take in a young boy found shipwrecked on the beach. He turns out to be a very talented musician, played by Daniel Brühl, who was well established as an actor in Germany, and he worked really hard. We never saw him socially, because every single minute of every day when he wasn't filming he was having to learn the violin — the fingering if not the actual playing, which was dubbed in by Joshua Bell in the end, with a lovely score by Nigel Hess.

We had to go to Shepperton studios to shoot one scene, when they were filming *Phantom of the Opera* on another stage. Somebody asked me, 'Would you like to come in and see this wonderful theatre we've built?' and Maggie said, 'Don't take her, she'll want to buy it!' Nobody ever lets me forget my extravagant gesture in storing that theatre from *Shakespeare in Love*.

When *Ladies in Lavender* came out one critic moaned, 'This film will only appeal to fans of Maggie Smith and Judi Dench,' so we just hoped that there were enough of them to make it a success for Charles. The last I heard he was still trying to find backing for his next film, which he richly deserves to do.

A rather different director came to see me during the run of *The Royal Family* about making a very different kind of film. The American actor-director Vin Diesel arrived at the Haymarket, bringing so many flowers which they couldn't even get up the stairs, and certainly couldn't have got in the dressing room. He wanted me to be in his latest science fiction fantasy *The Chronicles of Riddick,* and unlike Charles he didn't seem to have any problems over the money. There were incredible sets, the like of which I had never seen: huge, vast sets on many, many stages. I went out to Vancouver, ostensibly for a week, and eventually stayed there for three weeks.

I never really understood the film, but I got to do that thing which I have always longed to do in a play, where somebody says something to you and suddenly your face goes into a mass of cracks, and then you collapse into a tiny little pile of china. I kept doing that a lot, materialising and then disappearing. They filmed me against a green screen with green spots all over my face, and I never quite knew what was going on. The film has still not been released in Britain, though it did get a late-night showing on television, and I wouldn't have missed the opportunity of making it.

I always want to do something completely different next, and *Pride and Prejudice* was in a very different mood. In that film I played Lady Catherine de Burgh, and the location for my home was Burleigh House, near Stamford, which is a glorious town. Barbara Leigh-Hunt had played the same part so brilliantly in the earlier television version that I rang her up and said, 'I'm just going to copy you.' But I think we were quite different in the end. Joe Wright directed it, and he hired the real butler at Burleigh to play the butler in the film. Harvey Pascoe was a lovely man, and he kept us on our toes about all the etiquette. He fell into the job absolutely, so much so that I think he gave up butling to become an actor.

Lady Catherine de Burgh was a very strong character, and so was my next film part in *Mrs Henderson Presents*. She was the lady who owned the celebrated Windmill Theatre, and I went to see some of the girls who had appeared there, now in their nineties, but still fantastically glamorous. They told me how extraordinary Mrs Henderson was, how wonderful she was to the girls, how she brought them food, and paid for their weddings, she really took them on as a family.

Her husband had died, and her son was killed in the Great War, and then she did this amazing thing of buying a theatre, which she knew nothing at all about. She hired Vivian Van Damm to run it for her, and her relationship with him was often confrontational. He was played by Bob Hoskins, whom I had never worked with before, and we had a lot of laughs. We had a terrible time dancing. Bob said, 'The trouble with you is you have hooves instead of feet!' When Van Damm bans her from her own theatre, she disguises herself as a man, and a Chinese lady, and as a bear. When people said to me, 'Was it you in the bear?' I said, 'Of course, why do you think I would not be in the bear's costume?'

Stephen Frears was directing, and I had so enjoyed working with him on *Going Gently* and *Saigon — Year of the Cat* that I was always going round to knock on his door and ask if he had got another job for me. We had a scene where I flew in a Tiger Moth, and they kept shooting us racing along the runway without ever taking off. They did it so many times that I said, 'This is ridiculous, it's like being interrupted in the middle of making love, we have to take off.' So we did, and sailed around over Henley, and back down again. I had to wear one of those leather caps like the Red Baron, and the whole thing was absolutely thrilling. That is when filming is wonderful, because suddenly you get to do something you have never done before, and I love to learn something new every day. It was like that shot in *The Importance of Being Earnest* of us firing arrows at a target; that was something that I had never done before, and always wanted to.

After a string of films in period costume I went back to my role as 'M' in *Casino Royale,* this time with a new James Bond, played by Daniel Craig. He is very different from Pierce Brosnan, but both are very good actors with an enormous sense of humour, and that is really important. I think you have got to be a bit self-deprecating as Bond; if you take yourself too seriously in it, or in anything really, it isn't good. Daniel is hugely good fun to work with, and he does most of his stunts himself.

I had always complained before that I never got to any of the foreign locations, and now I went twice — to Prague and then to Panama. When we arrived in Panama we were given an information pack, and when it was translated it said, 'the name of the street where you are filming means "get out of here if you can".' Somebody got shot, then there was a riot the next day when some policemen got kneecapped, and everybody threw a lot of bricks.

So we were all told to stay in for a day, then we were back there filming again. After a week they said, 'That's Judi wrapped, she's going home,' and everyone else said, 'Can I go home too?' It was terrible to feel right there on the edge of South America and not go on to explore the rest of it. I was very pleased to come home, but at the same time I thought it would have been wonderful to go on and visit lots of marvellous places I would have loved to see.

■ ■ ■ ■

20
MORE NAUGHTY
LADIES
2006–2009

■ ■ ■ ■

The year 2006 was a strenuous one for me both on film and on stage. *Notes on a Scandal* was physically demanding as well as quite emotionally draining. My knee was giving me trouble, and some of the location shots were up several flights of stairs. I was playing this terrifying schoolteacher, Barbara Covett, and I have always had a terrible fear of a mass of schoolchildren together, which I just had to get over, as the first day's shooting was in a school in North London. Fortunately the children all turned out to be lovely, both interesting and interested, and very enthusiastic.

I had read the book some time before, and found the story fascinating. Patrick Marber did a very sensitive adaptation for the screen, but I did have a big argument with him about one scene, when the young schoolteacher Sheba was going through Barbara's drawers looking for the diaries, and it said 'she goes through her grey bras and pants'. I said that, just because Barbara was this rather dodgy character, somebody you might not like to ask round to tea, she doesn't have grey bras and pants, she doesn't necessarily have to live in a dingy flat. I was concerned that she looked right, and we tried lots of different looks for her. In the end, I thought that what we did get was absolutely right.

Barbara is attracted to the new teacher played by Cate Blanchett, who she discovers is having an affair with one of the boys. Her jealousy prompts her to expose the relationship, which shocks the school, the boy's parents and the teacher's husband, played by Bill Nighy. She is deeply attached to her cat, Portia, and I had lots of scenes with it. One day I was sitting there, waiting to do something, and looked down and saw another cat basket. I said, 'That's not my cat's, what's that basket there?' They said, 'That's the stunt cat.' The stunt cat looked nothing like the cat I was using, it was a huge big chap.

I was shooting one scene and Richard Eyre said to me, 'You can probably go and have a sit down for twenty minutes because the next scene is just the cat running to the door, pausing, looking back at you, startled, and then running off.' I said, 'Then I'll take a couple of months off.' But the stunt cat never got a chance, the ordinary cat did it. Then after all that, you didn't see much of the ordinary cat either in the end.

The young actor playing the boy who has the affair had a difficult part, but he did it with the most enormous charm, and his father was with him all the time. Andrew Simpson was sixteen, and he had just got five A-levels, and one felt one ought to say, 'Don't be an actor, stay with going to law school.' But he was such a good actor, and Cate and he worked fantastically well together, because it was quite uncomfortable for her, they had some quite explicit scenes, which I thought were really delicately done.

After that, it was a great relief to return to Noël Coward, and go back to John Gielgud's old dressing room at the beautifully kept Haymarket Theatre again too. We all had a glorious time doing *Hay Fever* — his plays are such fun to do. Back in the Sixties, doing *Private Lives* with Edward Woodward had been like going to a marvellous party every night, and I felt exactly the same about playing Judith Bliss in *Hay Fever* forty years later, even though Coward's lines are as difficult to learn as Oscar Wilde's or David Hare's. This very theatrical family

343

behave so badly to the guests they invite down to the country that it was an invitation I found irresistible.

Edith Evans had preceded me in this part too, at the National Theatre in the Sixties, and the actress who had created the part of Judith Bliss in the theatre was the formidable Marie Tempest. I have a lovely letter framed at home which her grand-daughter wrote to me, in which she said that Marie Tempest always paused at the door at her first entrance in each act, until there was huge applause. Then she would come on and get on with the play. She would do another little scene and have another entrance, and do it again, to huge applause. She said her brother used to slide to the floor in embarrassment.

Noël Coward was always a stickler for having his lines spoken exactly as he had written them, and I think he was absolutely right, you should respect the author's creativity. So when Greg Doran asked me to play Mistress Quickly in a musical version of *The Merry Wives of Windsor* I was a little anxious, until I found to my relief that it was all Shakespeare's text that had been set to music. Nothing was added, just a few things subtracted, and Paul Englishby wrote the most beautiful score.

One of the most rewarding things about that show was that it brought in a whole new audience for Shakespeare because it was a musical, just as Trevor Nunn had done with his musical version of *The Comedy of Errors*. At the stage door there would be really young people saying that they had never been there before, and that they had had a lovely time. If it didn't have quite the same appeal to some of the older traditionalists, it certainly seemed to for that younger generation. I hope it brought them in to see plays without music in them, other Shakespeare plays.

We all had a very larky time. We did it in a straight run all over the Christmas period, we had a ball, and I think the audience did too. Mistress Quickly did a series of amazing cartwheels across the front at one point, though some people had the temerity to suggest it wasn't me in that costume. Greg had another brilliant sight gag for me. The set was a line of houses diminishing in size to give perspective, which created the right illusion until I walked on from the back of the stage and looked down on the rooftops. It is the first time I have ever felt really tall. It was almost hallucinogenic, and I had this sudden thought that Mistress Quickly had been at the mushrooms.

The cast included Haydn Gwynne as Mistress Page, Alexandra Gilbreath as Mistress Ford, my brother Jeff as Robert Shallow, and my regular cabaret partner Brendan O'Hea as Pistol. Desmond Barrit was playing Falstaff, but after about four weeks of rehearsal and learning all the songs, he had to have an operation on his toe, which meant giving up the part. So Simon Callow took over at almost the last minute. He told us that he was filming on a beach in Greece when he got the phone call from Greg. He thought he heard him ask if he would come to Stratford to take over the RSC, so he had said yes before he realised what the offer really was. It was hard for him, because there were only about ten days' rehearsal left, but he did a remarkable job in such a short time.

I like working with directors I know and trust, such as Peter Hall, Trevor Nunn and Richard Eyre, but I also enjoy working for the first time with the younger directors like Sam Mendes, and one of the main reasons I agreed to be in *Madame de Sade* in 2008 was for the chance to work with Michael Grandage. He had made such a success of running the Donmar that he took over the much bigger Wyndham's Theatre for a season of *Ivanov* with Kenneth Branagh,

Twelfth Night with Derek Jacobi, *Hamlet* with Jude Law, and the *de Sade* play.

Michael had asked me to be in it a long time before, he very much wanted to do the play, and I wanted to do it for him. It was fiendishly difficult. Indeed it was without doubt the most difficult play I have ever done — and do I regret it? No, not a single day of it, because if there is such a thing as a learning curve, my goodness I learnt it through those few months at Wyndham's.

I thought it was a terribly difficult story to tell: difficult language, difficult translation from the Japanese, beautiful clothes — but we couldn't get into the dressing rooms in them, never off the stage. There were so many really difficult things, and actually to capture the audience in that play was like scaling Everest every night, and sometimes scaling Everest twice a day. But I wouldn't have missed it, because it required the most incredible discipline.

Brendan O'Hea came to it and said to me afterwards, 'Well, you just come on apologising for the play. Do stop that,' and it made a big difference to me. I thought, Yes, that's exactly what I am doing.

Madame de Sade had an all-female cast of six — the other five were Rosamund Pike, Frances Barber, Deborah Findlay, Jenny

Galloway and Fiona Button. We happened to be rehearsing in the same building as the all-male cast of *Waiting for Godot* — Ian McKellen, Patrick Stewart, Simon Callow and Ronald Pickup, all of whom I knew, so the opportunity of sending them up seemed irresistible. The very first day that we were there, when they had been rehearsing for some time, we opened their door and looked in appalled, shut the door again and ran away. Then, because of the nature of our play, we just found a very rude word every day to write on a piece of paper and slip under their door — words that I have never heard before, and I don't expect ever to hear again.

The production was beautifully designed, and Michael Grandage was a joy to work with, but the script was difficult to learn, and on the first night I cut a page and a half. Actors are so kind when you do something like that, and Frances and Deborah said afterwards, 'You see, it didn't matter at all, they're all told the story anyway.' But you just feel as if you are falling backwards into a black hole, because the audience never go so quiet as when they know an actor has dried; the silence is deadly.

That is quite different from the stillness when an audience is held, where the company and the audience can completely become one thing. That is more difficult now, because people watch more television, and I think that an audience doesn't realise how amazingly restless it can be. What drives me mad are those digital watches, where I can tell during the run if I am doing it quicker or not, and I start to wonder if I am going to beat the watches on this one. You also know exactly where the coughers are.

I am so often asked, 'Does the audience make any difference?' Of course! It is the only reason you bother to be in the theatre, in order that tonight it can be better than last night, that you can crack something that you haven't yet, that this audience will be quieter, that this audience really will at the end think they have had a marvellous experience, and you have told the author's story. I always get that very depressed feeling at the end, and then miraculously a night's sleep somehow prepares you for doing it a step up the next day.

My Michael loved to quote Ralph Richardson, who said to him when they were shooting a scene in *Eagle in a Cage,* a film about Napoleon on St Helena: 'Acting is a strange business, my boy. One day it's there, and the next day nowhere to be seen.' None of us really knows the recipe for the marvellous thing that can happen on very rare occasions, but I know what the recipe isn't. The recipe isn't to have a long night's sleep, get up and have a bath, do something in the morning, eat a very light lunch, go to bed for an hour and a half in the afternoon, go to the theatre feeling like it, put on your make-up, go on and then find that you just fall a thousand feet, when you simply can't do anything right.

I also know that the recipe can be that you work all day on another play, you arrive at the theatre exhausted or tired, you try and sleep and you can't, you get up, you put the make-up on, you think, I don't know how I am going to get through it . . . And something happens.

We didn't get very good notices for *Madame de Sade,* which I usually try to shrug off and forget, but I was very cross with the critic of the *Daily Telegraph* who used his review not just to attack that play, but launched into a criticism of me in several previous parts. I broke the habit of a lifetime and wrote to him: 'I used to admire you, but now I realise you are a C. S., Charles Spencer — Complete Shit.' He wrote back to say he was not a complete shit: 'I love my wife and I'm kind to my cat.'

But despite our reviews the whole Donmar season at the Wyndham's Theatre was virtually sold out, with a huge advance booking, so it was a great success for Michael Grandage.

After the decadence that was the subject of that play, I found myself in the very different nineteenth-century moral atmosphere portrayed by Mrs Gaskell in *Cranford,* whose novels were adapted for television by Heidi Thomas. This BBC series contained a formidable cast of ladies, including Eileen Atkins, Francesca Annis, Emma Fielding, Deborah Findlay, Barbara Flynn, Lesley Manville, Julia McKenzie and Imelda Staunton. The men were a quite impressive lot too, including Jim Carter, Michael Gambon, Philip Glenister, Alex Jennings, Martin Shaw and Greg Wise. It seemed like a cast of thousands.

It was a five-part series, and we had an unbelievably tight schedule for the filming. I worked out that in the last three weeks I was doing an average of seven scenes a day. For the cinema, one scene would take at least a day, or if it was a very complicated scene it would take more than a day. But these days, in television, things have to get faster and faster, because there isn't the money. So you are very conscious of the fact that if you don't know your lines you are wasting money. But everyone did arrive word-perfect. I had an hour's car journey each way, and that is a great time to learn lines.

Fortunately, we did have rehearsal time for *Cranford;* we had dance rehearsals, and we were taught a lot about the etiquette of the time. The historian Jenny Uglow gave us a wonderful lecture about the 1840s and the coming of the Industrial Revolution, she told us what that little town of Knutsford would have been like then, which was absolutely invaluable to us. Unlike the weather we endured on the filming of *Mrs Brown* and *Iris,* we had the most gloriously hot sunshine in April.

I had not acted with Eileen Atkins since we had been together in *Hilda Lessways,* an adaptation of Arnold Bennett's *Clayhanger,* in 1959 — live TV, if you have been through that, you have been through fire. In *Cranford* I had a lifesize cutout figure made of her, which we used to bring out every now and again, in scenes after her character had died, and stand her amongst us, to see if anyone would notice. The director Simon Curtis never noticed the first time we did it on a railway station. The producer, Sue Birtwistle, arranged to have photographs taken every time we got it out, and we sent them to Eileen. I think she got the cutout in the end, I do hope she did, and that she kept it.

The locations were in Lacock in Wiltshire and Ashridge in Hertfordshire, and then I was back in West Wycombe again. Most of the interiors were shot in the studio, when Sue Birtwistle came to my aid; she went to such great lengths to ensure that we were all well looked after. Following all the exertions in *The Merry Wives* I had to have a knee operation, and just two weeks after I had had it done I fell over the dog's bone at home and cracked something in my other ankle. I was limping about everywhere, holding on to two people on every possible occasion.

So Sue got me a motorised scooter, which was absolute heaven, and much envied, because we had so many changes and I had a little way to go to my dressing room. I whizzed back and forth, but I wasn't allowed to do more than eight miles an hour. The crew thought I might have done, so when no one was looking they put fines on it, and parking notices, and I had *Hell's Angels* written on the back. But I couldn't have done it otherwise, because I was in a lot of pain.

The calls were early; I was up at 5.15 a.m., and not back home until 8 or 9 p.m. Of course, you get used to that kind of schedule, but that is why it is so much nicer filming in the summer than the winter, when sometimes you never actually see daylight at all. You go out in the dark, you come home in the dark, and you are inside all the time, like a house plant; but in the summer it is much easier to get up on a beautiful morning.

The series was so popular with the audience that the BBC decided to make two more ninety-minute specials for Christmas 2009. It took some while to plan, as it was difficult to sort out the availability of all the original cast at the same time. I had another unfortunate accident during the filming of the *Cranford* sequel too. On my way home one evening a fox suddenly ran across the road, and as my driver stamped on the brake I was thrown forward and banged my head on the seat in front. It gave me the most enormous black eye, and the director took one look at it and sent me home for a week to recover. After all, it would have been distinctly out of character for the respectable Miss Matty suddenly to appear on screen looking as if she had been in a fight.

■ ■ ■ ■

21
AND FURTHERMORE
2009–2010

■ ■ ■ ■

The two films in which I appeared in 2009
could hardly have been more different in
scale or approach. The first was *Nine,* a
musical based on Fellini's film *8 1/2,* which
was originally done on stage on Broadway
in 1982 with Raul Julia, and here at the
Donmar in 1996. That production was then
revived on Broadway in 2003 with Antonio
Banderas and Chita Rivera. The film was
directed by Rob Marshall, who previously
made *Chicago.* We started working on it in
August 2008, and we had a hugely good
time, but it had its frightening moments.
There were great musical numbers in it that
we had to learn, and then go out on to the
set and rehearse with a lot of dancers, who
were all beautiful, stick-thin, and Italian.
Daniel Day-Lewis played the character
based on Fellini, and all the women in his
life were played by an international cast —
Sophia Loren, Nicole Kidman, Penelope

Cruz, Kate Hudson, Marion Cotillard, Fergie the American rock-singer with the Black-Eyed Peas, and me.

We worked on the songs and everything else in the rehearsal room, and the studio set for the first day's shooting was a wonderful stage with seats for an audience. We were setting the scene with me singing it for Rob, with some of the dancers. We had been rehearsing for about four weeks, so I knew the song and the moves, and we were just about to start when Rob looked up and said, 'Oh, Sophia's arrived, you must come and meet her.' She is an absolute heroine of mine, and I said I would love to. After we met, Dan came in, and several of the others, and we all had a coffee together, it was a great thrill, and a feeling of excitement.

Then Rob said, 'We must go and do this work.' We walked away, and just as we were about to begin I looked up, and Sophia had walked in and sat in the front row with Dan Day-Lewis and stayed there. I said to Rob, 'It can never be more frightening than this moment, actually filming it can't be more frightening than this moment.' But it seemed to go well, and actually the most wearing part was the promotion we all had to do for it when it came out in December 2009. It now seems to be a standard requirement with a big-budget movie for the cast to have to go to America and talk about it. Nicole Kidman and I were doing a string of interviews together, one after the other, and one young man said to me, 'So it's mothers' parts now, is it?' I snapped back, 'Well, perhaps that's better than grandmother's parts!' Then he said to Nicole, 'You're very tall in this film.' She didn't answer anything at all to that, and then the publicity assistant said, 'I think it's time you left.' I came home for a week, then had to fly back out for the premiere. After all that promotion, the film didn't seem to make much of an impression with either the critics or the cinema-going public, rather to my surprise.

The second film, *Rage,* was virtually shot on a shoestring, but the director was Sally Potter, who is no slouch when it comes to filming. It was a series of monologues, shot in a tiny room against a coloured screen, and Sally just sat opposite us with the camera. I had to roll a joint in it, and Sally got this wonderful boy in from university, who showed me how to do it with just one hand. I only did two or three days' filming, and I never met any of the others in the cast, which included Eddie Izzard and Jude Law. *Rage* had what must be one of the strangest premieres ever — it was projected on to the outside of the British Film Institute on the South Bank on 24 September 2009, but I think it also had a few normal screenings in cinemas.

In early 2010 I returned to one of my very favourite parts, which I had last played forty-five years ago — Titania in *A Midsummer Night's Dream* — and for the same director, Peter Hall. The attraction for me was that it went back to 1962 and my association with Peter. He said, 'Look, I'm going to be eighty that year, can we do this?' It was extraordinary, I did remember every single word of the whole play. I was exhausted at the end of the evening, because not only was I saying my part, but I found myself saying everybody else's parts too.

It was produced at the new Kingston Rose Theatre, where the stage design replicated the one from Shakespeare's Rose Theatre. Peter's idea was that I should play Titania as Queen Elizabeth I, with her distinctive red wig and white ruff, because the play was likely to have been performed at her court, and was part of a repertoire of plays she would have seen.

We did a kind of dumb-show at the beginning, and tried it first with Elizabeth on her throne, and Oberon as the Earl of Essex, but I thought it was essential to show just a group of actors getting ready. At first I used to take the scroll with the script from somebody who didn't play anything in it, as if Elizabeth came on and actually edged somebody aside, but then I realised that tells another story. So we all thought up the eventual opening together.

Because I was still word-perfect in the part, I started rehearsals a week after the rest of the cast. What was so uncanny for me was hearing Rachael Stirling as Helena, the part her mother Diana Rigg had played with the RSC when we did it before. She was different of course, but sometimes she sounded so like Diana. It brought back other memories of that 1962 production — when John Gielgud brought Peggy Ashcroft to see it, and I hadn't known he was there until he sent me the most huge bouquet of beautiful white flowers, with a note, 'I felt I could fly away with you.'

This time I played some scenes quite differently. When Bottom was wearing the ass's head, he laughed with a hee-haw, so I hee-hawed back. That just happened one day in rehearsal. I thought, If she loves him so much she wants to try and speak like him too, why ever not? I thought at the end we ought to have had a very small fairy with an ass's head run across the stage, I was frightfully keen on that idea, but there was no money to do that, and of course that too would have told another story.

It is only now that I have realised what it is about *The Dream* which always appeals to people. It is because an audience loves to know something that the cast doesn't know, just before it happens, and of course in this play Shakespeare sets it all up. He tells you everything, so the audience are always one step ahead, and I am sure that is part of the delight of it.

We did a special children's matinee at the Rose, and they just loved it. At the Coutts Sponsors' reception afterwards, somebody said to me, 'Oh, you all look as if you are having such fun.' I thought that proved that when we all enjoy each other's company it transmits itself to an audience. It is not that we are going out there thinking what fun we are all having, but doing it to convey this glorious story. It was a really happy, good company, and it was great being at the Rose too, it is such a lovely theatre, and I just want it to go from strength to strength.

I am always saying that I want each job to be as different from the last one as possible, and in my ideal world I would like to alternate regularly between working on stage and on film, either for television or the cinema. But it rarely seems to work out like that, and in recent years I have spent more time in front of the camera than in the theatre. I am more comfortable with the discipline and routine of live theatre, and am grateful that that is where I learnt my trade.

When I was at Central I had a problem with projection, and one of the teachers, Oliver Reynolds, said to me, 'Maybe it's because you're such a small girl that you have a small voice,' so that set up a real challenge for me. But first Michael Benthall at the Old Vic, and later Frank Hauser at Oxford, certainly cured me of that vocal shortcoming.

Today a lot of young actors have no intention of going on the stage. What they want to do is make a hit in television, or make a film, and have that kind of life. But I think those of us who have had a theatre training are very lucky, because the biggest projection you have got to do is in the theatre, then comes television, and then comes film. If you want to shrug your shoulders on a film you can just think it, and it would be picked up in your eyes. But actors who have only ever done television or film can get caught out by not projecting enough if then they come to do a play in the theatre.

Some young actors write to me, and others come to see me, and that is lovely, though I can't ever think what parallel lines they draw with me. I find I learn so much from people who are much younger now. I am always flattered when a young director asks me to work for them, and if young actors want to know things it is rather rewarding, because then I feel I am passing something on. I don't want to impose it on them, but if they are interested and want to know about verse-speaking or whatever it is, that I can do.

I do think it is a terrible pity that so many of them don't know who Peggy Ashcroft was, or Ralph Richardson; I feel it is so important that we keep the memories of our predecessors alive, and know about the work of David Garrick, Sarah Siddons, Henry Irving, Ellen Terry, Alec Guinness and Sid Field. We should all have a curiosity about the profession, and what we have come from. Those great figures of my early years do seem now of Mount Rushmore proportions, but maybe that's just to us who learnt at their knees. I love that mystery surrounding certain actors, and of course we don't have that any more. When you walk on to a stage in the theatre now, and it says clearly in the programme 'Definitely no photographs', you are faced with a hundred little red lights, and you know that they are taking your picture on a camcorder or a mobile phone.

On a film you have to sit and answer questions about what you think of the part, why you wanted to play the part, and I think that's none of the public's business. Why should you know the ins and outs of everything? You don't say to a dress designer like Betty Jackson, 'Why have you made a dress like that? Why did you cut the dress like that?' Why should the public know everything? The joy of the theatre is not really going and knowing that somebody had terrible difficulty playing this part, or why they did it; it is to go and be told a story, the author's story, through the best means possible. In any case, I never know why I've done something, it's for lots of reasons. I want to keep a quiet portion inside that is my own business, and not anybody else's.

To those who are just starting out on their careers, I advise them not to do it at all if there is anything else they want to do. I also advise them that they mustn't do it if they haven't got great reserves of energy, because there is no point if you are a tired person. As I have got older I am conscious that I take more care to conserve my energy, and

I have a routine when I am in a play that hardly varies.

I get up at about 8.15, almost on the dot, and I pad about in a dressing gown a lot. When you have a performance that day, you are conscious of it from the moment you open your eyes. Then I do all the things I have to do — shop, make lunch, do the washing, though I no longer do the ironing, someone does that for me, which is the greatest luxury. If I am being driven in, I sleep in the car, but I always get there early; Michael used to say that that was because I am so nosy, I have to know about everybody. I like to know that people are all right, and I like to catch up with what has been going on while I am not there. We have to be there by the half, but I get in at about 5.30. I just have to be there, and I have to shed off home, and stop worrying about all the things I haven't done.

If the play is in repertoire, and we haven't done it for several days, then we have to do a word-run, which is essential, but can be very tedious. Rehearsing it after we have opened is such agony. We are all so pleased to see each other, but then we have to sit there and go right through the whole play — oh, that is so tedious.

I find that I always have to do the same

things before a performance. My dresser makes me a cup of tea without any milk, but with honey in it, and then I steam my voice, which is something I have always done since *A Little Night Music*. A steamer is like a teapot, with a spout but no handle, it has a cork and a long tube. You fill it half full of boiling water, put your mouth to the spout and breathe in and out without taking your mouth away. It is just wonderful, and lots of singers do it. Then I take a phial of ginseng and royal jelly, which is just like drinking pure honey. I always have one before each performance, matinee and evening, I wouldn't feel right if I didn't have that. I do vocal exercises, such as chanting 'hip-bath, hip-bath', and I have the tannoy on all the time, unless I am sharing a dressing room with Anna Massey, who can't bear to hear the audience coming in, and we compromise on just the last five minutes before curtain-up.

I used to be able to go out to tea after a matinee, but I can't do that any longer. I don't like to break the continuity of the theatre. I don't even go to the canteen between two shows unless it is for something very, very special, like the day John Gielgud came to see *Amy's View* at the National. Instead, I just have something light in my dressing room: potted shrimps or a bit of chicken — although I was really spoilt when I was playing at Wyndham's Theatre. Michael and Finty gave me a present of a lobster salad sent in every night from Sheekey's Restaurant just down the alleyway, I can still remember how delicious that was. I had the same thing when I played next door at the Albery, now the Noël Coward Theatre. After that meal I sleep. My dresser wakes me with the cup of tea and the ginseng phial, and I am off again.

I love the repertoire system, I like to be employed but I don't like to be working every night. Michael used to give me the occasional little talk about taking it more easily, but I have never wanted to do that, there are not enough hours in the day for me. He also used to say that we should live each day as if it is the last, and I have always shared that view, as long as I can remember.

You do see people who work towards an age, and then at sixty or sixty-five you see them go into a deep decline, and you wonder: Why? What do you retire for? You retire if you are in a job that has just kept you employed, and given you some kind of income, and then you retire to do things that you really want to do. Well, I am doing the things I want to do now, so I don't want to retire. Actors are really remarkable people to be with. I like the company of other people, but I *love* the company of actors, and to be in a company. My idea of hell would be a one-woman show, I wouldn't be able to do that, I wouldn't know who to get ready for. The whole idea of a group of people coming together and working to one end somehow is very appealing to me. It is the thing I have always wanted to do, and I am lucky enough to be doing it. You don't need to retire as an actor, there are all those parts you can play lying in bed, or in a wheelchair.

What I want to do now is to be a tad more choosy. I want to do something that is much more unlikely for me, more daring, and if I am going to put my energy into a play, then I will do something I haven't tackled before. (Although if anyone came up to me and said, 'Would you do *Absolute Hell,*' of course I would do it.)

I have read a couple of new plays recently which I thought were good plays, but not for me. I have never done a Stoppard, never done a modern American play. I quite like not knowing what I will be offered, and being a bit uncertain about it. I would love to go to New York again for a short time, if it was the right thing for me to do. I made some terrific friends, and the whole of that theatre scene is so compact and intense. You all go and eat in the same area, so you meet actors who are in other plays, and you absorb the whole of the theatre scene in New York when you are there.

There is still so much I want to do, and I pray that I will be given the chance, and the time to do it. I treasure all the friends I have made through my work, and I look forward to making new ones in the future.

ACKNOWLEDGEMENTS

I am eternally grateful to all my friends and colleagues in the profession who have made my career such a happy and fulfilling one; many of them are named in these pages, and to the many others who are not I proffer my apologies as well as my thanks. Sadly some of them are no longer with us, and I miss them all.

For their permission to quote them, my particular thanks to John Moffatt for his poem, to David Hare for his letter, and to Trevor Nunn for his Address at my husband Michael's funeral. I am also grateful to John Miller for his help, not least in checking many of the details against my occasionally patchy memory. I would like to express my thanks to Ion Trewin for inviting me to write this book, for his patience when I hesitated about seeing it through to completion, and for his meticulous editing of the manuscript.

Finally, I must pay special tribute to my

daughter Finty and my grandson Sammy for all their love and support, and to whom I have dedicated *And Furthermore.*

Chronology of Parts

THEATRE

DATE	PLAY	ROLE	THEATRE
1957	York Mystery Plays	Virgin Mary	St Mary's Abbey

THE OLD VIC COMPANY, 1957–61

DATE	PLAY	ROLE	THEATRE
1957	*Hamlet*	Ophelia	Old Vic
	Measure for Measure	Juliet	Old Vic
	A Midsummer Night's Dream	First Fairy	Old Vic
1958	*Twelfth Night*	Maria	Old Vic
	Henry V	Katharine	Old Vic
	(Both plays also on tour to North America)		
1959	*The Double Dealer*	Cynthia	Old Vic
	As You Like It	Phebe	Old Vic
	The Importance of Being Earnest	Cecily	Old Vic
	The Merry Wives of Windsor	Anne Page	Old Vic
1960	*Richard II*	Queen	Old Vic
	Romeo and Juliet (Also Venice Festival)	Juliet	Old Vic
	She Stoops to Conquer	Kate Hardcastle	Old Vic
	A Midsummer Night's Dream	Hermia	Old Vic
	(And walk-ons in *King Lear* and *Henry VI*)		

THE ROYAL SHAKESPEARE COMPANY, 1961–2

1961	The Cherry Orchard	Anya	Aldwych
1962	Measure for Measure	Isabella	Stratford
	A Midsummer Night's Dream	Titania	Stratford
	A Penny for a Song	Dorcas Bellboys	Aldwych

THE NOTTINGHAM PLAYHOUSE COMPANY, 1963

1963	Macbeth	Lady Macbeth	Nottingham
	Twelfth Night	Viola	Nottingham

(Both plays also on tour to West Africa)

	A Shot in the Dark	Josefa Lautenay	Lyric

THE OXFORD PLAYHOUSE COMPANY, 1964–5

1964	Three Sisters	Irina	Oxford
	The Twelfth Hour	Anna	Oxford
1965	The Alchemist	Dol Common	Oxford
	Romeo and Jeannette	Jeannette	Oxford
	The Firescreen	Jacqueline	Oxford

THE NOTTINGHAM PLAYHOUSE COMPANY, 1965–6

1965	Measure for Measure	Isabella	Nottingham
	Private Lives	Amanda	Nottingham
1966	The Country Wife	Margery Pinchwife	Nottingham
	The Astrakhan Coat	Barbara	Nottingham
	St Joan	Joan	Nottingham

THE OXFORD PLAYHOUSE COMPANY, 1966–7

1966	The Promise	Lika	Oxford
	The Rules of the Game	Silia	Oxford
1967	The Promise	Lika	Fortune
1968	Cabaret	Sally Bowles	Palace

THE ROYAL SHAKESPEARE COMPANY, 1969–71

1969	The Winter's Tale	Hermione/Perdita	Stratford
	Women Beware Women	Bianca	Stratford
	Twelfth Night	Viola	Stratford
1970	London Assurance	Grace Harkaway	Aldwych
	Major Barbara	Barbara Undershaft	Aldwych
1971	The Merchant of Venice	Portia	Stratford
	The Duchess of Malfi	Duchess	Stratford
	Toad of Toad Hall	Fieldmouse, Stoat and Mother Rabbit	Stratford
1973	Content to Whisper	Aurelia	Royal, York
	The Wolf	Vilma	Playhouse, Oxford
	(Also at Apollo, Queen's & New London)		
1974	The Good Companions	Miss Trant	Her Majesty's
1975	The Gay Lord Quex	Sophy Fullgarney	Albery

THE ROYAL SHAKESPEARE COMPANY, 1975–80

1975	Too True To Be Good	Sweetie Simpkins	Aldwych
1976	Much Ado About Nothing	Beatrice	Stratford
	Macbeth (Also Donmar and Young Vic)	Lady Macbeth	Stratford

	The Comedy of Errors	Adriana	Stratford
	King Lear	Regan	Stratford
1977	*Pillars of the Community*	Lona Hessel	Aldwych
1978	*The Way of the World*	Millamant	Aldwych
1979	*Cymbeline*	Imogen	Stratford
1980	*Juno and the Paycock*	Juno Boyle	Aldwych
1981	*A Village Wooing*	Young Woman	New End

THE NATIONAL THEATRE COMPANY, 1982

1982	*The Importance of Being Earnest*	Lady Bracknell	Lyttelton
	A Kind of Alaska	Deborah	Cottesloe
1983	*Pack of Lies*	Barbara Jackson	Lyric

THE ROYAL SHAKESPEARE COMPANY, 1984–5

1984	*Mother Courage*	Mother Courage	Barbican
1985	*Waste*	Amy O'Connell	Barbican and Lyric
1986	*Mr and Mrs Nobody*	Carrie Pooter	Garrick

THE NATIONAL THEATRE COMPANY, 1987–91

1987	*Antony and Cleopatra*	Cleopatra	Olivier
	Entertaining Strangers	Sarah Eldridge	Cottesloe
1989	*Hamlet*	Gertrude	Olivier
	The Cherry Orchard	Ranevskaya	Aldwych
1991	*The Plough and the Stars*	Bessie Burgess	Young Vic
	The Sea	Mrs Rafi	Lyttelton
1992	*Coriolanus*	Volumnia	Chichester

| 1992 | The Gift of the Gorgon | Helen Damson | Barbican and Wyndham's |

THE NATIONAL THEATRE COMPANY, 1994–8

1994	The Seagull	Arkadina	Olivier
1995	Absolute Hell	Christine Foskett	Lyttelton
	A Little Night Music	Desirée Armfeldt	Olivier
1997	Amy's View	Esme	Lyttelton
1998	Amy's View	Esme	Aldwych
	Filumena	Filumena	Piccadilly
1999	Amy's View	Esme	Barrymore, New York
2001	The Royal Family	Fanny Cavendish	Theatre Royal, Haymarket
2002	The Breath of Life	Frances	Theatre Royal, Haymarket
2003	All's Well That Ends Well	The Countess	Swan, Stratford-upon-Avon, and Gielgud
2006	Hay Fever	Judith Bliss	Theatre Royal, Haymarket
	The Merry Wives of Windsor	Mistress Quickly	RSC Stratford
2009	Madame de Sade	The Marquise	The Donmar at Wyndham's
2010	A Midsummer Night's Dream	Titania	Rose Theatre, Kingston

DIRECTOR

DATE	TITLE	COMPANY/VENUES
1988	*Much Ado About Nothing*	Renaissance Theatre Company
1989	*Look Back in Anger*	Renaissance Theatre Company
	Macbeth	Central School of Speech and Drama
1991	*The Boys from Syracuse*	Regent's Park Open Air Theatre
1993	*Romeo and Juliet*	Regent's Park Open Air Theatre

TELEVISION

DATE	TITLE	COMPANY
1959	*Family on Trial*	Associated Rediffusion
1960	*Z-Cars*	BBC
	Henry V – Age of Kings	BBC
1962	*Major Barbara*	BBC
1963	*The Funambulists*	ATV
1965	*Safety Man – Mogul*	BBC
1966	*Talking to a Stranger*	BBC
1968	*On Approval*	Yorkshire
1970	*Confession – Neighbours*	Granada
1972	*Luther*	BBC
1973	*Keep an Eye on Amelie*	BBC
1977	*The Comedy of Errors* (RSC)	Thames
1978	*Macbeth* (RSC)	Thames
	Langrishe, Go Down	BBC
	A Village Wooing	Yorkshire
1979	*On Giant's Shoulders*	BBC
	Love in a Cold Climate	Thames
1980–3	*A Fine Romance*	London Weekend
1980	*The Cherry Orchard*	BBC
	Going Gently	BBC

1982	Saigon – Year of the Cat	Thames
1985	The Browning Version	BBC
	Mr & Mrs Edgehill	BBC
	Ghosts	BBC
1986	Make and Break	BBC
1988	Behaving Badly	Channel Four
1990	Can You Hear Me Thinking?	BBC
	The Torch	BBC
1991	Absolute Hell	BBC
1991–2002	As Time Goes By	BBC
1999	The Last of the Blonde Bombshells	BBC
2007	Cranford Chronicles	BBC
2009	Cranford: Return to Cranford	BBC

FILMS

DATE	TITLE	DIRECTOR
1964	The Third Secret	Charles Crichton
1965	He Who Rides a Tiger	Charles Crichton
	A Study in Terror	James Hill
	Four in the Morning	Anthony Simmons
	A Midsummer Night's Dream	Peter Hall
1973	Dead Cert	Tony Richardson
1984	Wetherby	David Hare
1985	A Room with a View	James Ivory
1986	84 Charing Cross Road	David Jones
1987	A Handful of Dust	Charles Sturridge
1988	Henry V	Kenneth Branagh
1994	Jack and Sarah	Tim Sullivan
1995	GoldenEye	Martin Campbell
	Hamlet	Kenneth Branagh

1996	*Mrs Brown*	John Madden
1997	*Tomorrow Never Dies*	Roger Spottiswoode
1998	*Shakespeare in Love*	John Madden
1999	*Tea with Mussolini*	Franco Zeffirelli
	The World Is Not Enough	Michael Apted
2000	*Chocolat*	Lasse Hallström
2001	*The Shipping News*	Lasse Hallström
	Iris	Richard Eyre
	The Importance of Being Earnest	Oliver Parker
2002	*Die Another Day*	Lee Tamahori
2004	*Ladies in Lavender*	Charles Dance
	The Chronicles of Riddick	Vin Diesel
2005	*Pride and Prejudice*	Joe Wright
	Mrs Henderson Presents	Stephen Frears
	Notes on a Scandal	Richard Eyre
2006	*Doogal* (Voice only)	Dave Borthwick
	Casino Royale	Martin Campbell
2008	*Quantum of Solace*	Marc Forster
	Rage	Sally Potter
2009	*Nine*	Rob Marshall
2010	*Jane Eyre*	Cary Fukunaga

AWARDS

1961   Paladino D'Argentino at the Venice Festival for *Romeo and Juliet*

1965   BAFTA Award Most Promising Newcomer for *Four in the Morning*

1977   SWET Award Best Actress for *Macbeth*

1980   SWET Award Best Actress for *Juno and the Paycock*

1981   BAFTA Award Best Actress for *A Fine Romance* and *Going Gently*

1984   SWET Award Best Actress for *Pack of Lies*

1987   Olivier Award Best Actress for *Antony and Cleopatra*

1995   Olivier Award Best Actress for *Absolute Hell*

1995   Olivier Award Best Actress in a Musical for *A Little Night Music*

1998   Golden Globe Award Best Actress for *Mrs Brown*

1998　Critics Circle Award Best Actress for *Amy's View*

1998　BAFTA Award Best Actress for *Mrs Brown*

1999　Academy Award Best Supporting Actress for *Shakespeare in Love*

1999　Tony Award Best Actress for *Amy's View*

1999　American Shakespeare Guild JOHN GIELGUD AWARD for Excellence in the Dramatic Arts

2000　BAFTA Award Best Supporting Actress for *Shakespeare in Love*

2000　Golden Globe Award Best Actress for *The Last of the Blonde Bombshells*

2000　BAFTA Award Best Actress for *The Last of the Blonde Bombshells*

2001　BAFTA Award Best Actress for *Iris*

ABOUT THE AUTHOR

Dame Judi Dench is one of the foremost stage, screen, and television actors of our time. She won an Academy Award in 1999, was awarded the OBE in 1970, created a DBE in 1988 and a Companion of Honour in 2005.

The employees of Thorndike Press hope you have enjoyed this Large Print book. All our Thorndike, Wheeler, and Kennebec Large Print titles are designed for easy reading, and all our books are made to last. Other Thorndike Press Large Print books are available at your library, through selected bookstores, or directly from us.

For information about titles, please call:
(800) 223-1244

or visit our Web site at:
http://gale.cengage.com/thorndike

To share your comments, please write:
Publisher
Thorndike Press
10 Water St., Suite 310
Waterville, ME 04901